BizTalk 2013 EDI for Health Care

HIPAA-Compliant 834 (Enrollment) and 837 (Claims) Solutions

Mark Beckner

Apress

BizTalk 2013 EDI for Health Care: HIPAA-Compliant 834 (Enrollment) and 837 (Claims) Solutions

An Apress Advanced Book

ISBN-13 (pbk): 978-1-4302-6607-5

ISBN-13 (electronic): 978-1-4302-6608-2

Trademarked names, logos, and images may appear in this book. Rather than use a trademark symbol with every occurrence of a trademarked name, logo, or image we use the names, logos, and images only in an editorial fashion and to the benefit of the trademark owner, with no intention of infringement of the trademark.

The use in this publication of trade names, trademarks, service marks, and similar terms, even if they are not identified as such, is not to be taken as an expression of opinion as to whether or not they are subject to proprietary rights.

While the advice and information in this book are believed to be true and accurate at the date of publication, neither the authors nor the editors nor the publisher can accept any legal responsibility for any errors or omissions that may be made. The publisher makes no warranty, express or implied, with respect to the material contained herein.

President and Publisher: Paul Manning

Lead Editor: Steve Weiss

Editorial Board: Steve Anglin, Mark Beckner, Ewan Buckingham, Gary Cornell, Louise Corrigan, James T. DeWolf, Jonathan Gennick, Jonathan Hassell, Robert Hutchinson, Michelle Lowman, James Markham, Matthew Moodie, Jeff Olson, Jeffrey Pepper, Douglas Pundick, Ben Renow-Clarke, Dominic Shakeshaft, Gwenan Spearing, Matt Wade, Steve Weiss

Coordinating Editor: Anamika Panchoo

Copy Editor: Lori Cavanaugh

Compositor: SPi Global

Indexer: SPi Global

Artist: SPi Global

Cover Designer: Anna Ishchenko

Distributed to the book trade worldwide by Springer Science+Business Media New York, 233 Spring Street, 6th Floor, New York, NY 10013. Phone 1-800-SPRINGER, fax (201) 348-4505, e-mail orders-ny@springer-sbm.com, or visit www.springeronline.com.

For information on translations, please e-mail rights@apress.com, or visit www.apress.com.

Apress and friends of ED books may be purchased in bulk for academic, corporate, or promotional use. eBook versions and licenses are also available for most titles. For more information, reference our Special Bulk Sales–eBook Licensing web page at www.apress.com/bulk-sales.

To my boys: may you stay healthy and insured and not have your information transported in an 834.

—Mark Beckner

Contents at a Glance

Contents

About the Author

Mark Beckner is a technical consultant specializing in business strategy and enterprise application integration. He runs his own consulting firm, Inotek Consulting Group, LLC, delivering innovative solutions to large corporations and small businesses. His projects have included engagements with numerous clients throughout the United States, and range in nature from strategy and business architecture to development of complete integration solutions. He has authored *BizTalk 2013 EDI for Supply Chain Management, BizTalk Recipes, Pro EDI in BizTalk Server 2006 R2*, and *Pro RFID in BizTalk Server 2009*, and has spoken at a number of venues, including Microsoft TechEd. In addition to BizTalk, he works with Microsoft Dynamics CRM, SharePoint, and custom .NET development. Beckner, his wife Sara, and his boys Ciro and Iyer Blue live somewhere in the rugged deserts and/or mountains of the American West. His website is http://www.inotekgroup.com, and he can be contacted directly at mbeckner@inotekgroup.com.

Introduction

The Affordable Care Act (ACA) has had massive impacts on the health care industry, and many of today's headlines are directly related to the 834 EDI document type. All of the data integrations behind the highly visible federal and state exchanges start with enrollment and the maintenance (effectuation/reconciliation/etc.) of that enrollment data. When a user signs up for coverage via one of these websites, their data is transmitted to insurance providers using the 834 format. The 834 is ubiquitous within health care back-end systems, and knowledge of it is critical to an IT professional's ability to operate successfully within this industry. BizTalk provides an obvious integration platform and EDI engine for these types of integrations.

Specifically as it relates to 837s, there is an immense need within the claims management industry to build highly efficient EDI processing systems that are cost effective and easy to maintain and extend. BizTalk is emerging as the leading technology applied in this space due to its low initial cost and the relative ease with which it can be adopted into infrastructures that are Microsoft based. While the ramp-up to be highly proficient with the tool may be high, building your own fully HIPAA-compliant solution is completely achievable.

My objective in this book is to lay out a variety of patterns for implementing specific EDI Health Care—based BizTalk solutions, so that you—whether you are an executive, an architect, or a developer—can see all the components required and understand exactly what needs to be developed to build your own specific implementation. My hope is that you can accurately assess the skills required, the amount of time necessary, and the complexity of the tasks ahead, and that you can enter into the development of your solution with a clear idea of what is required to be successful.

A website dedicated to the application of BizTalk within the health care profession can be found at http://www.biztalkforhealthcare.com. You will find an array of topics, both technical and business focused, discussed on this site. You can also visit my site at http://www.inotekgroup.com.

Contacting the Author

If you have questions about the specifics of what it will take to successfully deliver your own EDI Health Care implementation with BizTalk Server, please contact me at mbeckner@inotekgroup.com.

Architectural Patterns

BizTalk is a development platform and lends itself to a wide variety of implementation styles. After you've worked with the platform on a number of projects, however, you will find that there are really only a few patterns that meet the critical requirements of a well-developed solution. You will look at the some of the most appropriate architectural patterns for health care implementations, centered on the specific requirements of the Professional Health Care Claim in the 837P 5010 format and the Benefit Enrollment and Maintenance in the 834 5010 format.

The Health Care Claim 837 Format

The 837 format is one of the most complex document types in EDI, and requires careful planning to implement correctly. By working through this document format in detail, you'll be able to quickly move on to other health care document formats without delay, as they will all follow similar patterns. The patterns you will look at include details on:

- Receiving inbound 837P files
    - Receiving data via SFTP, FTP, and AS2
    - Decrypting inbound data
    - Mapping to other 837P versions, proprietary flat file formats, and SQL Server databases
    - Returning acknowledgements
    - Working with orchestrations

- Sending outbound 837P files
    - Mapping from internal flat file formats
    - Creating source data from SQL Server
    - Encrypting data
    - Sending batched and unbatched data
    - Working with orchestrations

The Benefit Enrollment and Maintenance 834 Format

The 834 format is not as complex to map (in most cases) as the 837, but it does have a number of architectural requirements that are often required. In some cases, simply receiving the 834 and mapping to inbound data models is all that is required. In other cases, splitting the inbound data, doing business rule validation on it, and providing advanced metrics are required. The patterns you will look at specific to the 834 include details on:

- Receiving inbound 834 files
- Advanced pipeline development for 834 metrics and reporting, and for splitting inbound data
- Custom business rule development in an easy to maintain environment
- Advanced mapping for outbound 834 data

Receiving Inbound Data

Receiving and processing inbound data can take on a variety of flavors, depending on where the data is coming from, whether it is encrypted or not, what is being done with the data once BizTalk has it, and what kind of validation and acknowledgements are required. Some of the most common patterns to consuming this data and processing it are outlined in the following sections.

Receiving Data via SFTP

In many health care related businesses, data is exchanged using SFTP. SFTP ensures data is transferred in an encrypted format that allows for HIPAA compliant communication, yet is a simple to implement transfer protocol. Retrieving data via SFTP in BizTalk is very simple, and can be done through several adapters, none of which ship with the core product itself. Details on implementing two of these - the free bLogical adapter (available on CodePlex) and the new SFTP adapter that ships with BizTalk - are given in Chapter 5, "dapters, AS2 and Acks." The pattern for receiving the 837P data over SFTP is shown in Figure 1-1. And inbound 834 (and other document types) would follow a similar pattern.

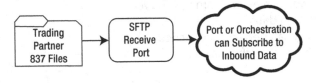

Figure 1-1. Receiving 837P data via an SFTP adapter

Receiving PGP Encrypted Data via FTP

When SFTP is not available, standard FTP is used; however, this protocol is not HIPAA compliant and requires the actual data file to be encrypted. FTP is very easy to implement within BizTalk through the use of the standard FTP adapter, but creating processes to decrypt the data is much more labor Intensive and requires coding. The most common approach to handling this is through developing a custom pipeline and pipeline component to do the decryption.

Details on building a decryption pipeline that can be used on an FTP Receive Port are given in Chapter 5. The pattern for receiving the 837P data over standard FTP and decrypting the data through a custom pipeline is shown in Figure 1-2. Again, 834 and other document types can be handled in a similar manner.

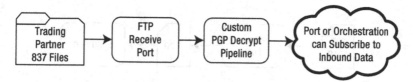

Figure 1-2. Receiving encrypted 837P data via the standard FTP adapter

Receiving Data via AS2

In some cases, data will be exchanged directly between trading partners using AS2. AS2 is a highly secure protocol that allows for various levels of encryption and signing of data. AS2 data is received over HTTP and requires the use of IIS and an HTTP adapter in BizTalk Server. Configuring AS2 is much more involved than is setting up other types of communication protocols, and can lead to fairly lengthy testing cycles with trading partners when used. Chapter 5 details how to implement an inbound AS2 solution. The pattern for receiving EDI data over AS2 is shown in Figure 1-3.

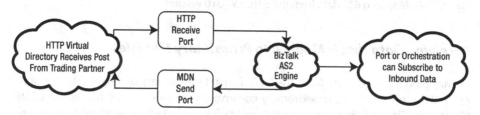

Figure 1-3. Receiving data via AS2

Receiving Data that is Mapped to Other Formats

Once data has been received via any protocol, something generally needs to be done with it. In many cases, it is mapped from the original standard into another version of the schema data which can be handled by legacy applications within an IT infrastructure. For example, with the release of version 5010, many companies have to exchange data in the 5010 format, but still have internal applications that deal with the data in the older 4010 version. These applications can directly consume 837P data, but are not 5010 compliant. Therefore, the inbound 837P 5010 format must be downgraded to the 4010 version through BizTalk mapping. Two patterns for receiving the 837P 5010 data and mapping it to the 4010 version is shown in Figure 1-4. One uses a simple Port to Port combination, while the other uses an orchestration to handle the mapping.

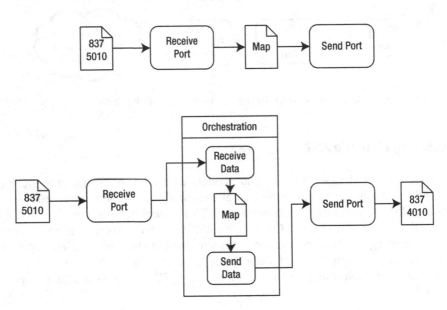

Figure 1-4. Mapping 837 data from the 5010 to 4010 version

Receiving Data that is Mapped to Proprietary Flat Files

Mapping inbound data from the 837P format (regardless of version) to a proprietary flat file format is also extremely common. One example of this is the ECSIF (Electronic Claims Submission Input Format) format, which is used by a wide variety of claims management systems. Mapping the 837P data to the ECSIF format (or other flat file format) often requires complex manipulations that are best handled with a combination of standard BizTalk mapping as well as XSLT. Chapter 4 "Mapping Data" has information on how to handle this mapping, and how to work with XSLT.

Receiving Data that is Mapped to a SQL Server Database

There are times when the inbound data simply needs to be received and sent directly to a database (or series of databases). There is a huge amount of data available in both the 834 and 837 formats, and writing this data to tables that reflect this structure in SQL server can require writing to dozens (or hundreds) of tables, along with many database lookups. There is really only one appropriate way to handle this kind of complexity within BizTalk, and it consists of a very simple pattern and the use of a stored procedure and XML.

For example, when the 837P data arrives in BizTalk, it is always converted to an XML structure that represents the EDI document. This XML can be passed directly to a SQL Server stored procedure which can tear apart the XML and insert it into the appropriate tables and databases. The pattern for receiving the 837P data and mapping it directly to a SQL Server database is shown in Figure 1-5, with some basic details of doing this for archiving data outlined in Chapter 2 "Solution: Receiving 837P Data."

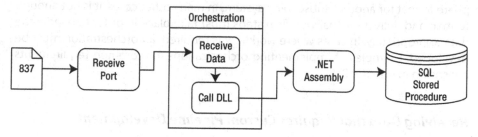

Figure 1-5. Mapping from an 837P to a SQL Server Database

Receiving Data that Requires an Acknowledgement

Acknowledgements come in several flavors. The 997/999 (Functional Acknowledgement) is the most common. The technical acknowledgement is also available, but is rarely used by trading partners. The MDN acknowledgement is specific to AS2. All of these acknowledgements are easily configured in BizTalk Server, and are automatically generated by the system when they are required. In the case of each of these a Send Port with an appropriate filter must be set up and certain fields may need to be configured in the Party and Agreement settings within BizTalk. Chapter 5 has details around working with the various acknowledgements. The pattern for sending acknowledgments for an 837 (834 is virtually the same) from BizTalk is shown in Figure 1-6.

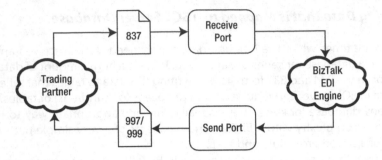

Figure 1-6. Sending Acknowledgements

Receiving Data that Requires an Orchestration

In many cases, there is no need for an orchestration in order to handle inbound 837P data - the data simply needs to be received, mapped, and dropped in an appropriate format for another subscribing system. In many other cases, it is not enough to map and deliver - actual workflow steps must take place in order to handle the data appropriately. In cases where workflow is required, an orchestration must be developed. Examples of implementing orchestrations for common requirements are shown in Chapter 2.

Receiving Data that Requires Custom Pipeline Development

There are frequently business requirements defined that require creative use of the various BizTalk components. One example of this is the 834 - with the way data is grouped, along plans, divisions, subscribers, and dependents, it is often a requirement to split the inbound data and to also perform counts and other metrics on the data (for reporting). This kind of work is often most easily done in the pipelines when the data is first received (and before anything arrives on the message box or instantiation of any orchestrations). Chapter 7 "Pipelines for 834 Processing" covers in detail how to set up a custom pipeline and pipeline component to split the data and to write metrics to the database. Figure 1-7 shows the flow of this data.

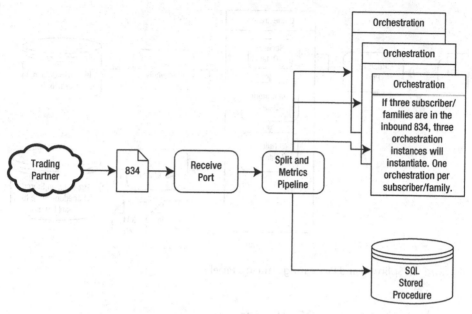

Figure 1-7. Splitting and Processing Data in a Pipeline

Receiving Data that Uses Custom Business Rules

Many organizations require that data validation occur prior to the acceptance of inbound data. The standard EDI schema validation and related 999 still occur, but additional custom validation of the data itself is required after this initial validation has passed. One important pattern related to this is the comparison of the inbound 834 data with existing historical data that is housed within an existing database. For example, if the requirement was to check and see if the first name, last name, or SSN has changed on an inbound subscriber or related dependents, then the inbound 834 data would need to be compared against the existing data. A detailed discussion about how this can be done using XML and a stored procedure is given in Chapter 8 "Custom Business Rules," while Figure 1-8 gives a conceptual overview. In this diagram, the historical data is pulled from Oracle in XML format, and then both this historical XML and the EDI 834 XML are passed as input parameters to a SQL Server stored procedure. The stored procedure does cross comparisons on the data, and inserts the results into tables for reporting, analysis, and further processing.

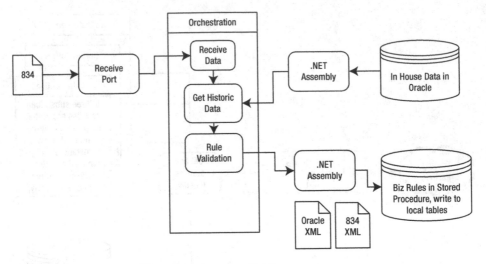

Figure 1-8. Splitting and Processing Data in a Pipeline

Sending Outbound 837P Files

We've looked at a variety of inbound patterns - now let's look at some outbound patterns. Sending data includes determining where the source data will come from, how this data will be mapped into the various EDI formats, whether this data will be batched or not, and how the data will ultimately be delivered. We'll look at a number of outbound patterns that will allow you to develop your outbound 834 and 837 solutions.

Sending Data Mapped from an Internal Flat File Format

Internal data is often stored by claims management systems, and this data can be readily exported in a variety of formats. In some cases, these systems can export fully compliant EDI documents. In other cases, these systems can export only proprietary representations of the claim data. In either case, this data generally must be mapped to the exact format and standard required by a trading partner. Some trading partners have very lax standards, while others have extremely rigid requirements.

> **Note** There are seven levels of HIPAA EDI Compliance. BizTalk handles level one and two.

In general, all trading partners have their own unique map from whatever internal format you have within your environment to their specific format. Even trading partners that have virtually identical EDI format requirements should have a separate map within BizTalk. The pattern for outbound maps based on an internal flat file format is shown in Figure 1-9.

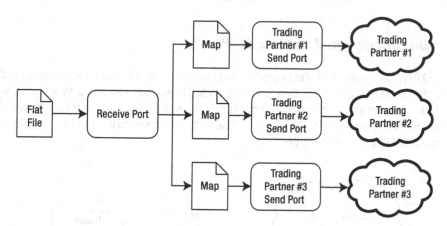

Figure 1-9. Mapping Outbound 837P Data from an Internal Flat File

Sending Data Mapped directly from SQL Server

Often, you can map your internal representation of data directly to a port (in XML) and map it to the target EDI standard without the use of an orchestration or other intermediary components.

For example, when claims data is available in SQL Server databases and tables, there is a fairly straightforward pattern that can be built which will allow this data to be structured for ease of mapping to 837P by a SQL stored procedure. This data can be retrieved from the stored procedure by BizTalk, mapped to the 837P format, and delivered.

The maps can often be extremely simple when using this pattern, as all of the data can be preprocessed and delivered to BizTalk by the stored procedure in the format required by the targeted trading partner. Instead of having logic in functoids and within the map, this logic can reside in SQL, and the maps can remain as simple as possible. Examples of building a stored procedure and mapping the contents to an outbound 837P are shown in Chapter 3 "Solution: Sending 837P Data." The pattern for handling this type of scenario is shown in Figure 1-10.

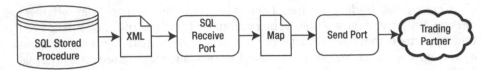

Figure 1-10. Mapping Outbound Data from SQL Server

Sending Unencrypted Data via SFTP

SFTP is a secure file transfer protocol, and files sent over SFTP can be unencrypted and still be HIPAA compliant. Sending files via SFTP requires a third party adapter, as BizTalk does not ship with an SFTP adapter. Chapter 5 gives details on how to work with one of the available SFTP adapters. The pattern for sending unencrypted 837P data via SFTP is shown in Figure 1-11.

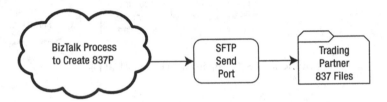

Figure 1-11. Sending Data via SFTP

Sending Encrypted Data via FTP

Data sent over the standard FTP protocol - which is very common within the health care world - must be encrypted for it to be HIPAA compliant. Encrypting data requires the use of a custom pipeline and custom pipeline component, which can be added directly to an FTP Send Port using the FTP adapter that ships with BizTalk. You can look at the discussions in Chapter 5 for more information on how to build out custom pipelines and pipeline components for encryption and decryption. The pattern for sending encrypted data via FTP is shown in Figure 1-12.

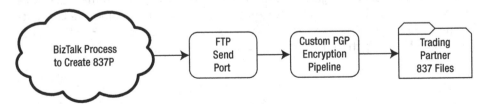

Figure 1-12. Sending Encrypted Data via Standard FTP

Sending Outbound Data Based on Inbound Data

A complex requirement that many companies face with the 834 is the need to base the outbound data mapping on what was originally contained on the inbound 834 data. This involves pulling current data from the internal data stores that represent the enrollment/effectuation data, along with pulling historical data related to the specific record from the original 834. The complexities associated with this can be managed through some smart mapping and extraction of data, and Chapter 9 "Advanced 834 Mapping" is dedicated to dealing with this specific concept. While it is a complex problem, the resulting component architecture can be relatively simple - most of the work can be done within a map, and there is no absolute requirement for an orchestration to complete this scenario.

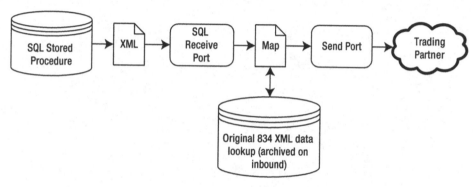

Figure 1-13. Sending Outbound Data Based on Inbound Data and Internal Data

Sending Batched Data

There are a number of options around batching data, the two most common examples for 837P being multiple claim records per ST/SE and single claim records per ST/SE. Trading partners will dictate their requirements around batching, including maximum number of claims in a file, maximum number of claims in a batch, maximum number of batches in a file, and so on. Dealing with these can often require major shifts in the way you build the same processes for different partners. For example, sending single claims per ST/SE will require a different set of maps and other components than will sending multiple claims per ST/SE. A detailed analysis and examples for implementing batching have been outlined in Chapter 3. While the examples in Chapter 3 are specific to the 837, the concepts all apply directly to the 834 and other data types.

Conclusion

There are a wide variety of patterns to dealing with EDI data. This chapter has outlined some of the most common or most useful, and has pointed to where in this book you'll be able to find more detail. In addition to the specifics around how to receive and send data via various protocols, how to encrypt and decrypt files, how to batch data and how to include orchestrations, you'll also need to know how to configure trading partners as BizTalk parties, and how to set up the core EDI functionality within BizTalk. In the next two chapters you will look at specific implementations of receiving and sending 837P data, both of which touch on many components of the various architectures just outlined. Chapter 6 outlines similar components specific to an inbound 834.

This chapter will walk through a complete end-to-end solution on how to build out BizTalk to receive 837P documents from an external trading partner and send an acknowledgement back. The data will be received via an SFTP adapter, archived, processed by an orchestration, and written to a flat file in the ECSIF format. This will introduce many of the key concepts required in virtually any environment that you may find yourself having to develop within.

The solution that you will be working through will demonstrate how to receive 837P documents from an external trading partner and send an acknowledgement back. The data will be received in unencrypted format on an SFTP site, archived by a BizTalk orchestration using a .NET library, and mapped to a flat file format. This will introduce many of the key concepts required in virtually any environment that you may find yourself having to develop within. The overview of this specific solution is shown in Figure 2-1.

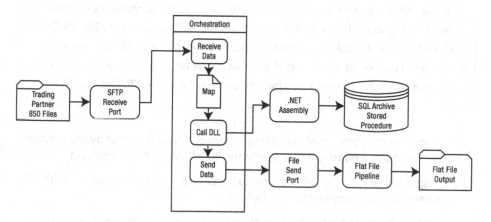

Figure 2-1. Inbound 837P Solution Overview

Visual Studio Solution

It is critical that your project structure and namespaces are correct from the start. If these are not exactly what you need for the proper architecture and organization of your solution, you'll be spending a great deal of time later in the process rewriting and retesting. For this solution, the namespace is in a structure that you should be able to use directly within your own solutions, substituting the wording, but not the structure. You will also be creating a Visual Studio project structure that will be generic enough to fit within any model you may find yourself confronted with. In the case of the solution being built out, the following Visual Studio projects and namespaces will be used:

- Solution Name: Company.BizTalk. This is a generic solution that can hold inbound and outbound projects (see Chapter 3, "Solution: Sending 837P Data"). There are several projects that are common to many projects, so having everything in one solution can be very helpful.

- Schemas. There are two schemas that will be used in this solution - the 837P 5010 schema that ships with BizTalk, and the proprietary ECSIF schema.
  - ° The 837P Schema will be contained in its own project. The project name for this will be Company.BizTalk.Schemas.X837P
  - ° The ECSIF schema will be contained in its own project. The project name for this will be Company.BizTalk.Schemas.ECSIF

■ **Note** When setting a namespace, never use a numeric value alone without at least one leading text character (such as the 837 in Company.BizTalk.Schemas.837), as it will result in a variety of potential naming conflicts, unexpected errors, and challenges in testing. If you wish to refer to an EDI document type directly in your namespace, use a pattern such as a leading "X", like X837P.

- Maps. The map project will contain all maps and XSLT required by the solution, and will have a namespace of Company.BizTalk.Maps.X837.Inbound

- Helper Library. There will be one external .NET assembly project with the namespace of Company.BizTalk.Helper

- Orchestration. There will be one orchestration used, which will be in its own project called Company.BizTalk.Orchestrations.X837.Inbound

- Pipeline. There will be one custom Send pipeline project, which will be called Company.BizTalk.Pipelines.X837.Outbound

The Schema Projects

There will be two schemas required for this project. The first is the 837P 5010 schema that ships with BizTalk. BizTalk has thousands of EDI schemas that come with it, crossing all of the document types and versions available. There are a number of 837P schemas, so it can be tricky to choose the right one when you are first getting started. Take the following steps to create a project that has the correct 837P BizTalk schema for your implementation:

- Create a new project in Visual Studio called Company.BizTalk.Schemas.X837P

- Find the HIPPA folder in the BizTalk EDI schema collection. There are two versions available - 4010 and 5010. You'll use the 5010 for this chapter. Click on the 837P folder and notice there is a "single" and a "multiple" available for selection. The schema you will need to use will depend on your batching requirements (if you have any).

If you are receiving a batched 837P, for example, which needs to be split into individual documents split at a certain level with access to claims, you would use the "multiple" version. Generally, the best approach is to start with the "single" version and if you find that batching is not working the way you would expect it to, experiment with the "multiple" version. Once you have found the correct XSD, add it to your Visual Studio schema project.

■ **Note**   To access the EDI schemas with BizTalk, browse to the root Microsoft BizTalk Server 2010 root folder and go to XSD_Schema\EDI. In this directory you will find a file called MicrosoftEdiXSDTemplates.exe. Running this file will extract all available schemas.

The second schema project will contain the proprietary ECSIF file schema structure. ECSIF files were very common on older claims management systems, and are a flat file structure, and will be referred to here and in several mapping discussions in this book. However, don't let this name mislead you - any flat file that you may need to create a schema for will follow the exact same pattern as what is required for the ECSIF - just substitute your flat file name where appropriate. An example of the ECSIF schema structure is shown in Figure 2-2.

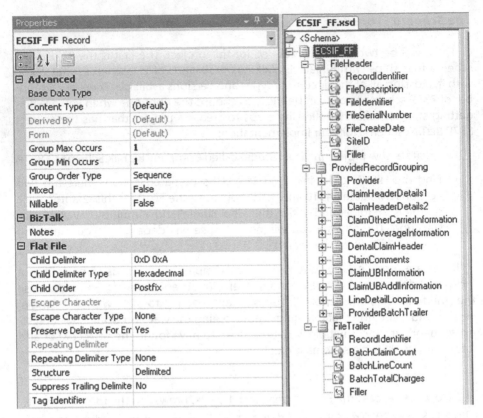

Figure 2-2. ECSIF Flat File Schema Structure Showing Child Delimiter

The steps required for the creation of the ECSIF project are as follows:

- Create a new project in Visual Studio called Company.BizTalk.Schemas.ECSIF

- Add a schema to your project that matches the flat file structure you are seeking. Any flat file schema that you may need to create can be created using BizTalk's Flat File Schema Wizard, available when you add a new item to your Visual Studio project and select Schema Files. The Wizard is pretty involved, and allows for virtually any structure, simple or complex; however, figuring out how to configure things to produce the schema you are seeking can be a challenge. There are a number of great resources available on the internet to help you work with this Wizard.

The schema projects (especially the X837P) are the foundation of many of the other projects you will be creating, as these other projects reference them. If the schemas change during the course of development, all of the other projects will be impacted. Do everything you can to get the schemas namespaced correctly, and structured correctly (you don't have to worry about the structure of the 837P schema, but you do have to deal with any schemas you are creating from scratch) at the start of your development.

The Map Project

The map project will allow for the mapping of the inbound 837P data into the ECSIF format. Because the ECSIF supports multiple claims, and the 837P contains multiple claims, there is no need for any splitting of the data before it arrives. The 837P data can simple be mapped into the target ECSIF format using whatever mapping techniques are required. That being said, mapping 837P data can be one of the most challenging mapping exercises that you will face. This is not because of BizTalk, but rather because of the enormity in size and structure of data that represent the claims within the 837P.

Chapter 4 ("Mapping Data") is dedicated to the activity of mapping, and looks at the specifics of what is required for the ECSIF (or other flat file) structure. Please refer to that chapter in order to build out the correct map.

The map project structure should be as follows:

- Create a new project in Visual Studio called Company.BizTalk.Maps.X837. Inbound

- Add a reference to the two schema project you have created, as you will be mapping from 837P to ECSIF

The .NET Helper Library Project

The .NET helper library is used by the orchestration to archive the inbound XML version of the EDI file to a database in its native XML format. This is an invaluable way of being able to access and report on data through SQL Business Intelligence (BI) platforms such as SSRS without having to push the 837P data to a traditional database model. The .NET class will have a single method in it that looks similar to the code shown in Listing 2-1. You can pass as many or as few parameters as you would like, depending on the needs of your reporting.

> **Note** Always mark your .NET classes as Serializable, so that they can be called from anywhere within BizTalk. To do this, type [Serializable] directly above the class declaration in your helper library.

Listing 2-1. Method Called from Orchestration to Archive Data to SQL

```
public void ArchiveInboundData(string strSourceFileName,
string
strTradingPartner, XmlDocument xmlSource, string
strConnectionString)
{
    SqlConnection sqlConnection = new
SqlConnection(strConnectionString);
    SqlCommand sqlCommand = sqlConnection.CreateCommand();
    sqlCommand.CommandText = "spInsertInboundData";
    sqlCommand.CommandType = CommandType.StoredProcedure;
    sqlConnection.Open();

    SqlParameter sqlParameter = new SqlParameter();

    sqlParameter.ParameterName = "@vchSourceFileName";
    sqlParameter.SqlDbType = SqlDbType.VarChar;
    sqlParameter.Direction = ParameterDirection.Input;
    sqlParameter.Value = strSourceFileName;
    sqlCommand.Parameters.Add(sqlParameter);

    sqlParameter = new SqlParameter();
    sqlParameter.ParameterName = "@vchTradingPartner";
    sqlParameter.SqlDbType = SqlDbType.VarChar;
    sqlParameter.Direction = ParameterDirection.Input;
    sqlParameter.Value = strTradingPartner;
    sqlCommand.Parameters.Add(sqlParameter);

    sqlParameter = new SqlParameter();
    sqlParameter.ParameterName = "@xmlSourceData";
    sqlParameter.SqlDbType = SqlDbType.Xml;
    sqlParameter.Direction = ParameterDirection.Input;
    sqlParameter.Value = new XmlNodeReader(xmlSource);
    sqlCommand.Parameters.Add(sqlParameter);

    sqlCommand.ExecuteNonQuery();
    sqlConnection.Close();
}
```

The stored procedure called from this method is shown in Listing 2-2. It simply takes the data passed to it and inserts it into a table. Once the data is in the table, it can be queried using standard T-SQL and XQuery. An example of querying the 837P XML data for the Clearing House Trace Number (a common unique identifier for submitted claims) is shown in Listing 2-3.

Listing 2-2. Stored Procedure to Archive 837P XML Data

```
CREATE PROCEDURE [spInsertInboundData]
    @vchSourceFileName As varchar(500)
    ,@vchTradingPartner As varchar(50)
    ,@xmlSourceData As xml
AS
BEGIN

    SET NOCOUNT ON;
    INSERT tblInboundData
    (
        vchSourceFileName
        ,vchTradingPartner
        ,xmlSourceData
        ,dtmCreateDate
    )
    VALUES
    (
        @vchSourceFileName
        ,@vchTradingPartner
        ,@xmlSourceData
        ,getdate()
    )
END
```

Listing 2-3. Using XQuery to Query Archived 837P XML

```
-- THE FOLLOWING WILL REMOVE NAMESPACE FOR EASE OF
QUERYING
SELECT CAST(REPLACE(CAST(@xmlSourceData As
varchar(max)),'ns0:',''))
 As xml) As SourceData
INTO #XML

-- THE FOLLOWING USES XQUERY TO RETRIEVE SPECIFIC VALUE
SELECT DCN.value('REF02__ClearinghouseTraceNumber[1]',
'varchar(255)') As DCN
FROM  #XML
CROSS APPLY SourceData.nodes('//REF_TS837Q1_2300_SubLoop')
As header(head)
CROSS APPLY head.nodes('REF_
ClaimIdentificationNumberForClearingHouses
 AndOtherTransmissionIntermediaries_TS837Q1_2300') as
DCN(DCN)
WHERE DCN.value('REF02__ClearinghouseTraceNumber[1]',
'varchar(255)') IS NOT
NULL
```

Once you have the .NET helper library built, you can reference the DLL in the orchestration project and call it to archive the inbound XML data. The next section shows how to call this referenced DLL from within an orchestration.

The Orchestration Project

In this solution, the orchestration will receive the 837P directly, map it, archive it to the database, and send it out in the final ECSIF format to a file directory. If archiving to the database was not a requirement, all of this could be accomplished without the use of an orchestration. The mapping could occur directly on either the Receive Port or Send Port. For this solution, however, the orchestration is used, and an example of it is shown in Figure 2-3. In order for this orchestration to work, you must add a reference to the .NET Helper DLL, the two schema projects, and the map project, all created earlier in this chapter.

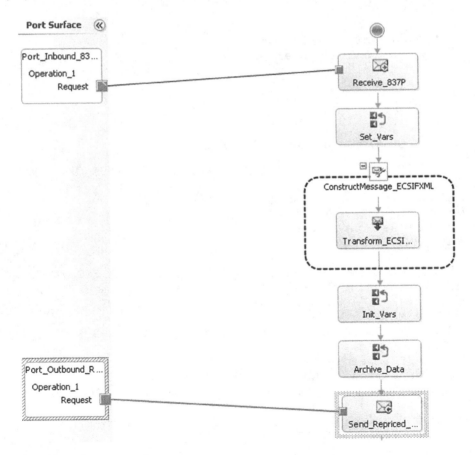

Figure 2-3. The Orchestration

Details behind each of the shapes in this orchestration must be given, as several of them are Expression Shapes and have important code behind them. There is no restriction as to how you populate your Expression Shapes, and no requirements as to naming standards. In the case of this orchestration, all of the Expression Shapes could be merged into one - but keeping them separate will allow you to see how you could add additional message types to this orchestration and be able to reuse common code. Figure 2-4 is a variation of the orchestration that shows receiving an additional document type of the 837I on a Listen shape and sharing the calls to the Init_Data and Archive_Data Expression Shapes.

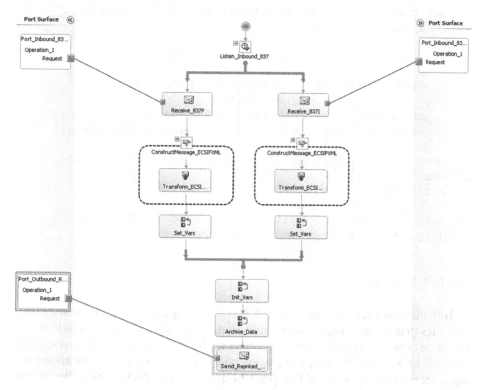

Figure 2-4. A Variation on the Orchestration with Shared Common Shapes

The Receive_837P Shape

This is a simple receive shape that must be set to an orchestration message type of the 837P schema (you'll need to add a reference to this schema project from your orchestration project). Call this message InboundData. The Activate property on this shape must be set to True.

The Set_Vars Shape

This shape sets variables that are specific to the document just received, and which are immediately available to the orchestration (as opposed to the Init_Vars shape which gets its data from a configuration file). The code behind this shape sets several of the fields that are passed as parameters to archive the data. The code, with notes, is shown in Listing 2-4.

Listing 2-4. Set_Vars Expression Shape Code

```
// Get the Trading Partner ID (from the party settings)
directly off the
// inbound file
strTradingPartnerID = msg837P(EDI.ISA06);

// Several options for getting the file name
strFileIdentifier = System.IO.Path.
GetFileName(msg837P(FILE.ReceivedFileName));
strReceivedFileName = msg837P(FILE.ReceivedFileName);

// getting the original inbound message as XML into a
parameter of type XML
// which can be passed into the helper class and written
to the database as XML
xmlOriginalEDI = new System.Xml.XmlDocument();
xmlOriginalEDI = (System.Xml.XmlDocument)msg837P;
```

The Init_Vars Shape

This shape is used to read from the BizTalk configuration file. There are often variables that are best kept configurable. In this case, the configurable field is the database connection string used to connect to the SQL Server database where the data will be archived. Adding a key/value pair to your configuration file allows for rapid access and alteration of this key. Using the BizTalk configuration file can be done as follows:

- Browse to the root BizTalk Server folder

- Open BTSNTSvc.exe.config in a plain text editor

- You can add new configurable fields to the <appSettings> node of this document. An example of storing a connection string would be:

```
<add key=" Company.BizTalk.Archiving.ConnectionString"
value="Data Source=BTSSQLSERVER;Initial Catalog=Archiving;
Integrated Security=SSPI;" />
```

- Save the modified config file and restart the BizTalk Host Instance. The field can now be referenced from an Expression Shape using the code shown in Listing 2-5.

Listing 2-5. Init_Vars Expression Shape Code

```
strConnectionString = System.Configuration.
ConfigurationSettings.AppSettings["Company.BizTalk.
Archiving.ConnectionString"];
```

The Archive_Data Shape

This shape calls the code in the .NET library to do the actual archiving, passing in several fields as parameters. These parameters include the source file name, the trading partner, and the data to be archived. The data being archived in this case is the XML version of the 837P data, readily available to the orchestration in the inbound message. The code for archiving is shown in Listing 2-6. Notice that the inbound message (which is the orchestration message of type Company.BizTalk. Schemas.X837P received on the Receive shape) can be converted to XML and sent straight in as a parameter.

Listing 2-6. Archive_Data Expression Shape Code

```
// the parameter shown here have all been set in previous
shapes
objHelper.ArchiveInboundData(strReceivedFileName,
strTradingPartnerID,(System.Xml.XmlDocument)
InboundData,strConnectionString);
```

The Pipeline Project

The final project required is a simple custom flat file pipeline using the Flat File Disassembler component that ships with BizTalk. The use of this pipeline on a Send Port will allow the outbound ECSIF document to be output in flat file format. The steps to create this pipeline are as follows, and the pipeline is shown in Figure 2-5.

- Create a new project called Company.BizTalk.Pipelines.X837.Outbound.

- Add a new Send Pipeline to this project.

- In the pipeline GUI interface, drop a Flat File Disassembler component on the Disassemble stage.

- In the properties of the disassembler component, set the Document Schema property to the Company.BizTalk.Schemas.ECSIF schema created earlier in this project (you may have to deploy the schema DLL in order to have access to this).

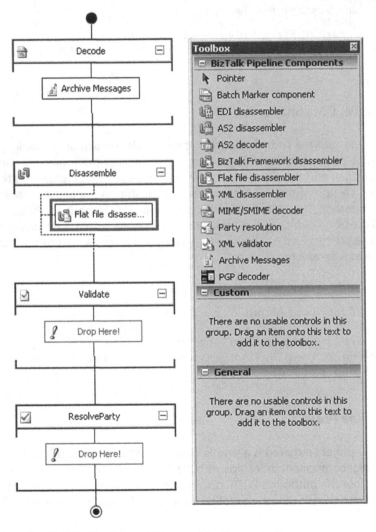

Figure 2-5. The Flat File Pipeline and Disassembler Component

Setting up the BizTalk Components

With all of the Visual Studio projects completed, you will have a number of BizTalk components to deploy and configure. The first step will be to deploy the DLLs that are created when you compile your Visual Studio projects. This can be done in a variety of ways, but the one which will allow you the most control (and is the quickest) is as follows. This can be used for adding new DLLs and for updating existing DLLs. After you deploy, always restart the BizTalk Host Instance.

- Open BizTalk Administration Console and browse to the Application where your code will be deployed. If one doesn't exist, create one called "Company. BizTalk"

- Right click the Application and select Add and then BizTalk Assemblies.

- In the window that opens, Click the Add button and add all of the assemblies for this solution - two schema DLLs, one map DLL, one orchestration DLL, and the .NET helper DLL.

- Click the Overwrite all checkbox.

- Click on each DLL and make sure the first and third checkbox in the Option window is selected for each one. You must do this for every DLL that you are adding. Figure 2-6 shows the checkboxes being set (the first and third also need to be checked for the .NET assembly, though it will have several additional boxes).

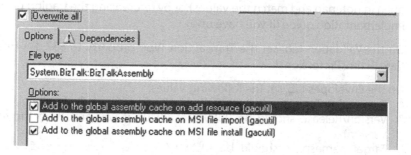

Figure 2-6. The Options to Select when Deploying Assemblies

> ■ **Note**   It can be helpful to have all of your Visual Studio projects write their compiled DLLs to the same directory, as you will be deploying them to BizTalk frequently for testing. This can be done by going into the project properties for each project and setting the Output Path of the build to a common directory, like a custom folder called Binaries.

Party Settings and Agreements

The steps to configure the BizTalk Party settings that contain all of the information about how the data will be validated and what the 837P envelope settings should be are as follows:

- Create a new BizTalk Party that represents your home organization. For now, this will be called Company. All you need to set is the name.

- Create a new BizTalk Party for your trading partner. This will be named Trading Partner for this solution. You'll need to set one Party up for every trading partner you will be doing business with. Only the name needs to be set.

- You will create one Agreement that represents the exchange of information between your trading partner and your company. Right click the Company Party and create a new Agreement. Set the Protocol type to X12, the First Party will automatically be set to Company, and the second Party should be set to your Trading Partner Party. The moment this is done, two additional tabs will appear within the Agreement. One tab is for inbound data from the trading partner to your company, while the other is for outbound data from your company to the trading partner.

- On the tab representing inbound data from the trading partner to your company, click on the Identifiers, Envelopes and Character set tabs and enter the appropriate information as required by the 837P envelope. You can easily access this either in a sample instance coming from the trading partner (just open in notepad and match the values) or by referencing the trading partner implementation guide (if you have one).

- On the Validation tab, set the Transaction Type property to 837_P - Health Care Claim: Professional.

- On the Envelopes tab, set the following values:
  - Transaction Type should be 837_P - Health Care Claim: Professional.
  - Version/Release should be 00501 (or 00401 if you are using the 4010 version)
  - Target namespace should be `http://schemas.microsoft.com/ BizTalk/EDI/X12/2006`
  - GS1 should be HC-Health Care Claim (837)
  - GS2, GS3, GS4, and GS5 should be set based on what your trading partner requires (again, see the trading partner implementation guide or a sample 837P instance from them)
  - GS7 should be X-Accredited Standards Committee X12
  - GS8 should be 005010X222.

> ■ **Note** The GS8 property value can be tricky to get right. If you are batching, or you have a trading partner that requires a certain value here, you may find that you have to create a custom pipeline to override this value right before it is sent to the trading partner.

The Receive Port

The inbound data will be received on an SFTP receive port. The details for configuring this port (with and without decrypted data) are given in Chapter 5. What is important to know here is that the port must not only be created, but must be bound to the orchestration. The steps for creating and binding this port are as follows:

- Create a Receive Port called Company.BizTalk.Receive.X837P.TradingPartner. This allows for a pattern that will support multiple trading partners, if needed.

- Add a Receive Location to this port and call it the same thing as the Receive Port. Make it of type SFTP and configure the appropriate settings for the SFTP connection. Since unencrypted 837P data will be received here, set the Receive pipeline to EdiReceive.

The File Send Port

The Send Port will be used to send the final ECSIF flat file which was mapped in the orchestration. The Send Port should be of type File, and should have the Send Pipeline property set to the Company.BizTalk.Pipelines.X837.Outbound pipeline created earlier. This Send Port should be called Company.BizTalk.Send.ECSIF.

Orchestration Binding

The orchestration is set to pick up a file of type 837P, map it to ECSIF, archive it, and then send out the ECSIF document. Once it has been deployed, it needs to be bound to the appropriate Receive and Send Ports. Take the following steps to bind the orchestration to the ports that were just created:

- In the BizTalk Administration Console, in the Application where you are working, click on the Orchestrations folder and open the Company.BizTalk. Orchestrations.X837.Inbound orchestration you have built and deployed.

- Click on the Bindings tab and set the Host property to the BizTalk Server Application host that is available.

- Set the Receive Port property to the Receive Port you created called Company. BizTalk.Receive.X837P.Receive.

- Set the Send Port property to the Send Port you created called Company. BizTalk.Send.ECSIF.

- Click OK to save these settings.

Enabling and Running the Solution

At this point, all of the components have been deployed and set up. All you need to do is enable your Receive Location for the inbound SFTP, start your Send Port for the outbound ECSIF flat file, and enable your orchestration. All of this can be done through the BizTalk Administration Console. Make sure and restart the BizTalk Host Instance so that all of the most current settings and assemblies are loaded into memory.

Conclusion

You have just worked through a full implementation for receiving 837P data and mapping it to an internal proprietary flat file format (ECSIF). Receiving data and getting it into your system is sometimes all there is to an implementation. Other times, sending data back out to trading partners is required. The next chapter focuses on a specific implementation of sending 837P data to a trading partner, and introduces a number of topics not covered in this chapter.

Solution: Sending 837P Data

The previous chapter looked at inbound 837P data. This chapter will look at outbound 837P data. It will introduce how to pull data from a source SQL Server database, map that data to an outbound 837P document, and batch the results into one file with multiple claims per ST/SE. There will be important information presented about how best to interact with SQL from BizTalk, how to structure the source data you'll be mapping from, and how to batch the data using configurations available in the BizTalk Party Agreement. The architectural overview of this solution is shown in Figure 3-1.

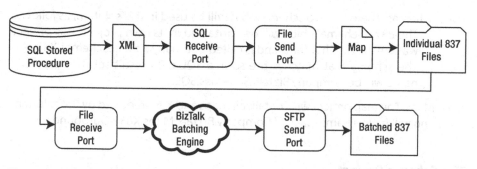

Figure 3-1. Outbound 837P Solution Overview

It is important to note here the pattern for batching. First, the data will be retrieved by a SQL Adapter, and then be sent out to a file directory by a Send Port in the 837P format. Over the course of a day, the SQL Adapter will run every hour, and during that hour all claims that may have stacked up will be retrieved and written out to a single 837P file. BizTalk batching will be set to trigger once a day, which means there could be up to 24 individual 837P files that will be written to the file directory and picked up by the batching Receive Port. When the BizTalk batch triggers, the 24 individual 837P files will be combined into a single 837P file with 24 ST/SE segments, each containing one or more records.

> ■ **Note** There are a wide variety of batching patterns that may be required and that can be built and configured in BizTalk with varying degrees of difficulty. This solution will demonstrate how to create one batched 837P file with multiple ST/SE segments containing one or more claim records.

Visual Studio Solution

As discussed in the previous chapter, namespaces and project structure are essential to a successful project, so always take time in the beginning to think through all of the components that will be required and how best to name and organize them. Trying to change namespaces and project organization later in the development cycle is especially frustrating with BizTalk, given the number of components and complexity of testing. For this solution, the following Visual Studio projects and namespaces will be used:

- Solution Name: Company.BizTalk. You can use the same solution you used for the project in Chapter 2.

- Schemas. There are two schemas that will be used in this solution, as follows:
  - The 837P Schema which will be contained in its own project. This project was created in Chapter 2, and is called Company.BizTalk.Schemas.X837P
  - The schema that matches the source SQL data result set. This project's name will be Company.BizTalk.Schemas.SQLData.

- Maps. The map project will contain all maps and XSLT required by the solution, and will have a namespace of Company.BizTalk.Maps.X837.Outbound

The Schema Projects

Two schemas are required for this project. The first is the 837P 5010 schema that ships with BizTalk, which was discussed in Chapter 2, "Solution: Receiving 837P Data". The second schema project will contain the schema which matches how data will be pulled from SQL Server. This is a structure that you have complete control over, and therefore should match as closely the structure of the outbound 837P schema as is possible.

The closer you are able to match the structure and hierarchy, the less complicated the mapping will be. You are not required to make it look the same, but the less effort you spend on creating a solid source structure that patterns your claim data properly, the more effort you will spend in mapping and creating code to get this claim data into the target EDI document.

In order to be able to define the schema for the source data coming from SQL, you'll want to work through the creation of a result set. The approach that allows for the most extensive flexibility around retrieving data, performing some level of data validation or cleansing, and formatting it in a "BizTalk friendly" way is through the use of a stored procedure.

If you have not used XML within SQL Server before, you are going to want to learn, as it is essential to building solid, easy to maintain solutions within BizTalk. The stored procedure that you will be using for this current solution is structured in the following way:

- Retrieve data directly from databases and structure it in a mapping ready format.

- Use FOR XML PATH to give a specific structure to the data and return the result set in XML.

- Use WITH XMLNAMESPACES to ensure it has a unique namespace and contains namespace prefixes that are immediately useable by a BizTalk Schema.

By using a stored procedure, you have endless options on structuring and returning data. You can use a single stored procedure to return data for all outbound trading partners, you can limit which trading partner is pulled at any given time through a parameter (or set of parameters), and you can apply specific logic to individual fields in order to prepare them for being delivered in the outbound 837P. An example of a stored procedure that can pull results in the XML format required by BizTalk is shown in Listing 3-1.

The actual structure of the data shown here is only to demonstrate how to write the procedure. You will want a much more robust and complex structure to the source XML which matches the requirements of what you will in order to successfully create the outbound 837P document.

Listing 3-1. An Example of a Stored Procedure to Return XML

```
CREATE PROCEDURE [dbo].[RetrieveClaimData]
-- namespace will be used within Schema and should match
your pattern
WITH XMLNAMESPACES('http://Company.BizTalk.SQLSource' as "ns0")
-- top level is set to NULL
SELECT NULL
        ,(SELECT c.Type As [ns0:ClaimType]
                ,c.Number As [ns0:ClaimNumber]
                ,c.ServiceDate As [ns0:ServiceDate]
                ,(SELECT p.ProviderFirstName As [ns0:FName]
                        ,p.ProviderLastName As [ns0:LName]
                        ,p.ProviderID As [ns0:BDate]
                FROM Providers p
                WHERE p.ID = c.ProviderID
                FOR XML PATH('ns0:Provider'), TYPE)
```

```
                        FROM SourceClaimInformation c
                        FOR XML PATH('ns0:Claim'), TYPE)
        FOR XML PATH('ns0:SQLSourceClaims'), TYPE
        END
```

Running this stored procedure from SQL Enterprise Manager will produce an XML document that can be used to generate your BizTalk schema, or you can create both manually. The creation of this stored procedure and the structuring of the outbound data should be the most difficult task that you have - not in development, but in business analysis and testing. If you get the structure right here, you will save a tremendous amount of time in the actual mapping and testing of data within BizTalk.

Once you have the source XML and schema structure worked out, you'll need to add it to a Visual Studio project. For this solution, it will be called Company.BizTalk.Schemas.SQLData.

The Map Project

You will have a single map for the outbound process, which will map the source data returned by SQL Server to the target 837P structure. Details for mapping the 837P are given in Chapter 4, "Mapping Data".

Note If you are delivering multiple document types - such as 837 Professional, Institutional, and Dental - out to multiple trading partners, you might want to explore the idea of mapping the source data from SQL Server to a canonical structure, and the canonical structure to the target 837P. In some cases, you can reduce overall long-term development through the use of a canonical schema, though short term it will increase development efforts and testing requirements.

The map project structure should be as follows:

- Create a new project in Visual Studio called Company.BizTalk.Maps.X837. Outbound

- Add a reference to the two schema projects you have created, as you will be mapping from the source SQL data to the 837P schema

Setting up the BizTalk Components

There are fewer Visual Studio components in this outbound solution, but there is more that must be configured within BizTalk, especially around the batch settings in the Party Agreement. You will need to set up a SQL Receive Port to pull the data from the stored procedure, a File Send Port to write this data out as an individual 837P, another Receive Port to pick it back up for batching, and a second Send Port to send the batched data when the BizTalk batch fires.

Before configuring these components, you will want to deploy your Visual Studio assemblies to the BizTalk Application. Steps for doing this are outlined in Chapter 2.

SQL Receive Port

The stored procedure that you created earlier in this chapter returns XML. Now you need to set up the Receive Port to pull this data into BizTalk. In general, interacting with SQL Server from BizTalk is best done through custom .NET components - the use of the SQL Adapters generally cause bloated, difficult to maintain solutions. However, in the case of pulling XML data from a stored procedure, you can use the SQL Adapter as a simple pass through mechanism that can be schedule to run on a periodic basis. You won't have to create any of the additional schemas that generally come with using the SQL adapter to retrieve data. The steps for setting up the SQL Receive Port and Receive Location are as follows (see Figure 3-2):

- Create a Receive Port called Company.BizTalk.Receive.SourceSQLXML.

- Add a Receive Location to this port and call it the same thing as the Receive Port. Make it of type SQL. Click on Configure next to the SQL Type, and set the following properties:
  - Poll While Data Found should be False
  - Polling Interval and Polling Unit of Measure should be values that represent how often you want to pull the data from SQL.
  - Connection String is the connection to the database where you stored procedure sits.
  - Document Root Element Name is a wrapped element that is used ONLY to allow for the adapter to pull the results. It will need to be the root node of your schema that you have created for the stored procedure results.

> **Note** The schema in Company.BizTalk.Schemas.SQLData should match exactly the structure of the XML returned by the stored procedure, except in that the root node must match what you set in the Document Root Element Name property. So, if the root node of your XML result set from the stored procedure is SQLSourceClaims, and the Document Root Element Name property is SQLRoot, then your schema will need to be SQLRoot/SQLSourceClaims. SQLRoot is just a wrapper node.

- ○ Document Target Namespace should match the namespace declared in your stored procedure and schema. In this case, it should be set to `http://Company.BizTalk.SQLSource`
- ○ The SQL Command is the full execute statement that you would use in SQL Enterprise Manager to run your stored procedure. If you have a parameter, you can specify it here. For example, to call the stored procedure that was created, this property would be set to "exec RetrieveClaimData". Or, if you had a parameter specifying the Trading Partner name to query, you could hard code it here as "exec RetrieveClaimData 'TPName'". In the case of a hardcoded parameter, you would want to create one SQL Receive Port per trading partner.
- ○ The URI can be set to anything, as long as it is unique. Something descriptive can be helpful, such as `SQL://SOURCEDB/EDI/TradingPartnerName.`

- Set the Receive Pipeline on the Receive Location to XMLReceive.

SQL Transport Properties	
⊟ Receive Configuration	
Poll While Data Found	**False**
Polling Interval	**60**
Polling Unit of Measure	**Minutes**
⊟ SQL Configuration	
Connection String	**Provider=SQLOLEDB.1;Password=**
Document Root Element Name	**SQLRoot**
Document Target Namespace	**http://Company.BizTalk.SQLSour**
SQL Command	**exec RetrieveClaimData**
URI	**SQL://SOURCEDB/EDI/TradingP**

Figure 3-2. The Configured SQL Receive Settings

Once you have the SQL Receive Port fully configured, you can enable it and immediately see data arriving on the BizTalk Message Box (assuming there are results available). You may not have a subscriber set up yet, so the data will suspend, but you'll know your data is being retrieved successfully.

File Send Port

The File Send Port is set up to push out a single 837P file whenever data comes in on the SQL adapter. This means that if the SQL Adapter is set up to trigger every 15 minutes, a file could be written every 15 minutes (assuming there is data returned). This File Send Port should be set up as follows:

- Create a Send Port called Company.BizTalk.Send.TradingPartnerName.X837P. Unbatched.

- Set the Send Pipeline to EdiSend.

- Set the Type to File and write this file to a directory on your computer.

- On the Outbound Maps tab, select the map you created in Company.BizTalk. Maps.X837.Outbound. The source and target document schemas should automatically be selected when you choose the map.

- On the Filters tab, set the following property: BTS.ReceivePortName == Company.BizTalk.Receive.SourceSQLXML

Starting this Send Port will now allow you to test that every time the SQL Receive Port returns data it get successfully mapped and transformed into an individual ST/SE 837P document. The actual batching of the data will happen in the following components.

File Receive Port

The second receive port in this pattern is the File Receive Port which picks up the individual 837P documents that are getting created each time the SQL Receive Port executes and returns data. When this File Receive Port picks up the data, the batching settings on the BizTalk Party Agreement will cause the document to queue up and not be delivered until the batch executes. Setting up this Receive Port can be done using the following steps:

- Create a new Receive Port and Receive Location combination, both named Company.BizTalk.Receive.TradingPartner.ToBeBatched.

- Set the Type to File and point it to the directory where the File Send Port is writing out the individual 837P files.

- Set the Receive Pipeline to EdiReceive.

■ **Note** There is no requirement that you design your batching outbound flow using this exact pattern of Send and Receive Ports. It is possible to batch without ever physically writing out the individual 837P documents to a file directory. However, by splitting the steps into smaller pieces, you'll find that development, testing, and troubleshooting are greatly simplified, since you have access to the document at all stages of the cycle.

SFTP Send Port

The final Port that will be created is the SFTP Send Port that delivers the batched data out to the trading partner. This Port needs to be configured in conjunction with the Batch configuration on the BizTalk Party - it references properties set in the configuration, and the configuration references this Send Port. The Send Port is covered first in this chapter, but you may want to develop them both at the same time using two BizTalk Administration Console windows.

The SFTP Send Port listens directly to the BizTalk Message Box for the batched 837P EDI file that was created when the Agreement's Batch triggered it (see the next section for details on this configuration). The Send Port uses several filters, and can be configured using the following steps:

- Create a new Send Port named Company.BizTalk.Receive.TradingPartner. Batched.

- Set the Type to SFTP. Details for configuring the SFTP adapter are given in Chapter 5, "Adapters, AS2 and Acks".

- Set the Send Pipeline to EdiSend, or to a custom pipeline that replaces the GS08 version with the appropriate value.

■ **Note** The GS08 and batching 837P 5010 documents has proved interesting. You may find that your data always fails batching due to a generic error. If you are certain that your configuration is correct, check the version in the GS08 on your outbound individual EDI document written by the File Send Port. If it is 005010X222A1, you may find that you need to set it to 005010X222 in the original outbound File Send and replace it with the correct value of 005010X222A1 in a custom pipeline on the final outbound SFTP Send Port. This is likely a bug in BizTalk Server batching, and may be corrected with a future patch.

- On the Filters tab, set the following filters:
  - ° EDI.ToBeBatched == false
  - ° EDI.BatchName == TradingPartner_Professional [should match the batch name configured in the Agreement]
  - ° EDI.DestinationPartyName == TradingPartner [should match the value of DestinationPartyName on the Identifiers tab of the BizTalk Agreement]

The final two bullets listed above are critical to the success of your batching. It can get very complicated when dealing with multiple document types across multiple parties that have various batch configurations. In the case of the solution at hand, the DestinationPartyName property on the Identifiers tab in the Agreement that contains the Batch settings is only set for batching purposes. You will not have set this property unless you are configuring batching. The values for both can be anything that you want them to be; they just have to match exactly with one another.

Batch Settings in the Party Agreement

In the previous chapter, you looked at configuring the base settings for the BizTalk Party and Agreement on inbound data. You don't need to configure any new parties or Agreements for the outbound solution, but you will need to configure these same settings on the tab that represents the outbound data, from the Company party to the Trading Partner party.

Once you have the envelope settings and various core settings configured (which should match almost exactly what you have for the inbound settings), you can look at configuring the actual batch - which is unique to this outbound solution. In order to configure the batch, open the Agreement you created in Chapter 2 and take these steps:

- On the Identifiers tab of the Agreement, set the DestinationPartyName to TradingPartner. This needs to be a unique value across all of your trading partners.

- On the Batch Configuration tab of the Agreement, click the New Batch button.

- Set the Batch name property to TradingPartner_Professional.

- Set the Batch filter property with the following filters:
  - ° BTS.ReceivePortName == Company.BizTalk.Receive.TradingPartner. ToBeBatched [this should match the name of the File Receive Port you created earlier in this chapter]
  - ° EDI.ST01 != 997

- Use the Scheduler to configure the appropriate outbound schedule. In the case of this solution, the batch should go out every 24 hours or once a day at a specific time. You can set this to whatever is required for your solution. When the specified time comes, if anything has queued up since the last time the batch executed then it will be immediately released.

> ■ **Note**   During development and testing, you will find that clicking the Override button on the Batch will be of great help. It forces a batch to be produced as soon as it is clicked.

- Click Start to allow the batch to begin processing. You may have to click OK or Apply and reopen the Agreement in order to get the batch to fully start. It can take several minutes the first time to get started.

- Check the running instances in your BizTalk Group Hub reports to ensure that your batch is started - you will see an orchestration running for every batch that you have started.

- Click on the Send Ports tab of the Agreement and select the SFTP Send Port you created earlier in this chapter - Company.BizTalk.Receive.TradingPartner. Batched.

- Click OK to save all of your settings.

> ■ **Note**   Getting the batch and Send Port to align with one another may take several stops and starts of the batch and of the BizTalk Host Instance. The batch functionality is pretty impressive, and it works great once it is running, but it can take some patience to get it right when you are first setting it up.

Enabling and Running the Solution

In order for this solution to work, both of the Receive Locations must be enabled, both of the Send Ports must be started, and the BizTalk Batch on the Agreement must be running. You will want to restart the BizTalk Host Instance to ensure that all of the most recent configurations and components are loaded into memory.

Conclusion

This chapter covered some critical aspects of developing BizTalk EDI solutions within the health care space. Most notably batching data and structuring your outbound data in SQL Server to prepare it for mapping. You will likely find that the requirements for your specific implementation vary from the specific pattern outlined in this solution, but you should have more than enough information now to be able to architect an efficient and highly maintainable outbound solution.

Mapping Data   Chapter 4

Constructing and deconstructing the data in the various EDI formats associated with health care is a task that requires both analysis and development skills. There are people within claims management who specialize in working with data as it is defined in the various formats, and someone acting as an EDI analyst will be critical during initial inbound and outbound BizTalk map implementations.

It is possible to look at an implementation guide and make intelligent decisions about how data should be mapped, but without the EDI analyst testing and reviewing the data, the chances of getting a fully compliant document that your trading partner will be able to consume is unlikely. To improve your chances for a compliant EDI document early in the development process, make sure to take the following steps:

- Whenever possible, get access to an actual EDI document that is being used for the specific trading partner you are working with. Implementation guides are good for reference, but as a developer, having access to the actual file is of immense value. It allows for side-by-side comparisons between what you are creating in BizTalk and what you know is a valid format.

- There are many alternative ways to populate data in the 837 Professional, Institutional, and Dental formats, and in the 834 enrollment, maintenance, reconciliation, and effectuation formats, and it is common to have mapping requirements that are unique to a trading partner. Be prepared to have maps that are very different between partners, whether inbound or outbound.

- Different trading partners require different levels of validation on data delivered to them. BizTalk officially supports level 1 and level 2 of HIPAA compliance validation (though it is arguable that levels 3 and 4 are met unofficially). If more levels of compliance are required, you will need to create your level 2 compliant document in BizTalk and then deliver the final file (individual or batched) to another application that will perform the additional levels of validation.

- The work of creating an outbound 834 or 837 document from scratch will likely require both a developer and an EDI Analyst. The developer will be focused on the BizTalk map implementation while the EDI Analyst will need to work with the developer to unit test the data. The testing portion of mapping health care EDI data, especially when dealing with the 837 formats, will take as much time as the actual development. Don't underestimate the need for this resource - only rarely will you find someone who can do both development and full analysis and testing of this type of data.

- In some cases, mapping is best done in multiple stages. It is always nice to be able to map a source document to the target EDI document (or vice versa) in a single map, but it does not always allow for the easiest or most maintainable solution. When developing your maps, think about the next person who may have to take these maps over from you at a later time. Will they be able to interpret what you have done and make modifications to it, if needed? When planning your mapping, think about ways to simplify your logic, and determine if creating several maps that take the data through several phases of transformation could ease your development.

The topics in this chapter will cover how to approach mapping the 834 and 837 formats (and mapping solutions in general) with several development techniques. While it isn't possible to demonstrate how to map either format in its entirety, it is possible to cover some key foundational information, and with some patience and (ideally) access to an EDI analyst, you will be able to create maps that are well architected and use the most appropriate mapping technologies.

> ■ **Note** When building outbound maps where you have control over the source data you are mapping from, try to pre-format as much data as possible (in the source flat file or database result set) so that once it gets to the BizTalk map, there is as little additional mapping needed as possible. The less complex your map is, the easier your solution will be to develop, test, and maintain.

BizTalk Mapping Technologies

There are several technologies that you will need to be very comfortable with in order to have the tools available in BizTalk to handle the complex mapping that is associated with working on 834 and 837 document implementations. The BizTalk

Visual Studio map is the canvas for development, but there are numerous options for mapping the data. These mapping technologies are as follows:

- Functoids. There are many functoids available to you, and it is possible to implement almost all of the 834 and 837 mapping requirements without the use of externals scripts. However, trying to implement an 837 map without the use of external scripts is a mistake, and will lead to an enormously complex map. Trying to support outbound 834 effectuation and reconciliation for integration with some trading partners without the use of external scripts is virtually impossible in many scenarios.

- Inline .NET code. The Scripting functoid in the mapper allows for a variety of script languages. You can accomplish quite a bit within these scripts, but you have limited access to libraries. Only those libraries available to XLANG can be used within a Scripting functoid, which is a subset of the overall .NET framework.

- External .NET Assemblies. When you need the power of the full .NET engine and associated libraries, you'll want to develop an actual assembly with methods that can be called from maps. Some tasks, such as interactions with a database, are often best done in external assemblies (as opposed to adapters).

- Inline XSLT. This is a very important skill to develop, and should not be overlooked or avoided. Tasks that could take many functoids or complex external .NET scripts can be done quickly using XSLT. Some mapping issues in more complex documents can't even be solved without the use of XSLT. While there will be some ramp up in learning this scripting language, it will be worth your time investment.

- External XSLT. In most cases, you will use the functoids and mapping options available in the map to complete your solution. In other cases, you may want to simply shell out to an external XSLT file to handle the mapping.

- SQL Stored Procedures. When dealing with business rules, data level transformations, or lookups, you may want to create stored procedures and deal with logic there. Calling a stored procedure through an external .NET assembly from a map is an easy architecture to build, and can be of great benefit.

Looking at actual examples of mapping technologies is what the rest of this chapter is devoted to. With these specific examples in front of you, you should be able to jump into the development of your 834 and 837 health care maps with a solid direction as to how to implement. You'll look at several examples - data being mapped to an outbound 837 and data being mapped from an inbound 834 and 837. Chapter 9, "Advanced 834 Mapping" covers how to map to an advanced form of the outbound 834.

Mapping to an Outbound 837

Mapping to an 837 from an internal data structure is required whenever you are sending outbound data. The solution outlined in Chapter 3 ("Solution: Sending 837P Data") discusses creating the internal data structure from an SQL Server stored procedure. However, source data can come from a variety of sources, including flat files, internal 837 documents, and various database structures, just to name a few. In the end, you will always be mapping from a source structure to the target 837 schema, and the mapping requirements will be similar regardless of the actual source of data.

Formatting Dates using an External .NET Assembly

There are a large number of date fields in an 837 document that have to be populated. Take the scenario where the source data was generated by SQL Server and all dates are in the format similar to 2012-10-21T04:00:20.043. The target date fields (such as BHT04) need to have this format converted to 20121021. This formatting must be applied to many fields, and the code used to convert from the SQL format to the EDI format needs to be used each time.

There are many options for implementation, including using standard functoids, but the most appropriate solution that uses the least amount of components is an external .NET assembly. If standard functoids were used, you would have to use several string functoids in a pattern, and this pattern would have to be applied over and over in the map. With the external .NET assembly, the code is written once, and a Scripting functoid is dropped wherever the conversion needs to take place. If the conversion logic needs to be changed for whatever reason (such as the source data format changes) then it only has to be changed in one place (the referenced DLL) and not everywhere the conversion is taking place (which would be the case with the functoid pattern).

In order to build this using an external .NET assembly, take the following steps.

MAPPING WITH AN EXTERNAL .NET ASSEMBLY

This exercise will walk through calling an external assembly to format dates in EDI compliant formats.

1. Create a .NET class library. Give it a namespace of Maps.Helper, and a class name of Helper.

2. Create a method called FormatDate which has one input parameter in string format. Write the code to convert from the source format to the target EDI format. An example of this code is shown in Listing 4-1.

3. Compile the assembly and reference it in your Visual Studio map project.

4. In the map, drop a Scripting functoid on the map surface. Drag the input from the source document's date field, and drop it on the target document's date field.

5. Open the Scripting functoid and click on the Script Functoid Configuration tab. Set the script type to External Assembly, then select your Script assembly, class, and method from the dropdowns. If your assembly is not shown, try closing Visual Studio and reopening. In some cases, you may have to install the DLL to the Global Assembly Cache (GAC - see next step) in order to be able to see it.

6. Test the map. This requires that the assembly be deployed to the GAC. Chapter 2, "Solution: Receiving 837P Data" discusses how to deploy assemblies via the BizTalk Administration Console, which places them in the GAC.

An example of the functoid being used on the BHT04 field is shown in Figure 4-1.

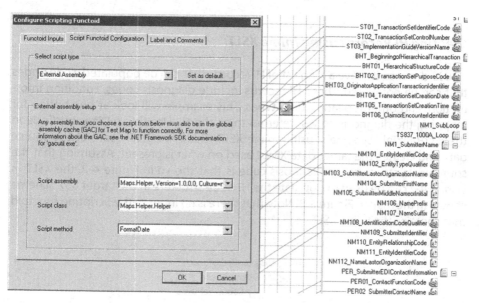

Figure 4-1. Calling an External Assembly from a Map

Listing 4-1. Formatting a Date

```
public string FormatDate(string dateString)
{
 if (string.IsNullOrEmpty(dateString) == false)
 {
 try
  {
   DateTime date = XmlConvert.ToDateTime(dateString,
   XmlDateTimeSerializationMode.Local);
   return date.ToString("yyyyMMdd");
  }
  catch
  {
   return string.Empty;
  }
 }
 else
 {
  return string.Empty;
 }
}
```

Creating HI Records using Inline XSLT

837 documents have a long list of HI records that can be populated, code nodes that can be populated. These HI records include diagnosis codes, condition information, and other repeating data types. This example will look at one option for mapping the diagnosis codes (referred to as the HI_HealthCareDiagnosisCode in the 837P BizTalk schema) - using Inline XSLT. The Inline XSLT looks at the source data and creates the target data XML based on what is present. Assuming that the source data structure for Diagnosis code is that shown in Figure 4-2, the XSLT in Listing 4-2 can be used to populate the HI node structure in the target 837 Schema shown in the map in Figure 4-3. Note that there is no input to the Scripting functoid that contains the Inline XSLT.

Figure 4-2. Diagnosis Code Structure in the Source Data

Listing 4-2. Inline XSLT for Diagnosis Code Creation

```
<xsl:element name="ns0:HI_HealthCareDiagnosisCode">
 <xsl:for-each select="//*[local-
name()='DiagnosisCode']">
  <xsl:if test="./@SequenceNumber = '1'">
   <xsl:element name="ns0:C022_
HealthCareCodeInformation">
    <xsl:element name="C02201_DiagnosisTypeCode">BK
</xsl:element>
     <xsl:element name="C02202_DiagnosisCode"><xsl:value-of
      select="translate(.,'.','')"/></xsl:element>
    </xsl:element>
   </xsl:if>

   <xsl:if test="./@SequenceNumber = '2'">
    <xsl:element name="ns0:C022_
HealthCareCodeInformation_2">
     <xsl:element name="C02201_DiagnosisTypeCode">BF
</xsl:element>
      <xsl:element name="C02202_DiagnosisCode"><xsl:value-of
       select="translate(.,'.','')"/></xsl:element>
     </xsl:element>
    </xsl:if>

   <xsl:if test="./@SequenceNumber = '3'">
    <xsl:element name="ns0:C022_
HealthCareCodeInformation_3">
     <xsl:element name="C02201_DiagnosisTypeCode">BF
</xsl:element>
      <xsl:element name="C02202_DiagnosisCode"><xsl:value-of
       select="translate(.,'.','')"/></xsl:element>
     </xsl:element>
    </xsl:if>
   </xsl:for-each>
</xsl:element>
```

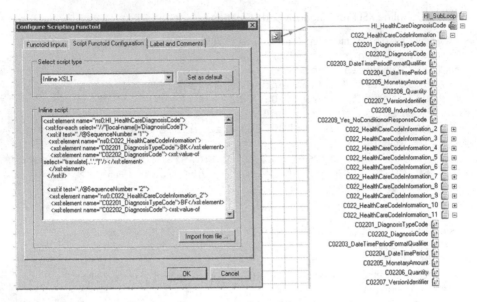

Figure 4-3. Mapping to the HI_HealthCareDiagnosisCode using Inline XSLT

What the XSLT is doing is looping through all of the source diagnosis codes that are available in the source data and creating target codes in the 837 EDI document in the exact XML structure that matches the schema. Depending on the SequenceNumber of the source code, the appropriate target code is created in the EDI document. The translate() method in the XSLT is used to remove periods from the source data before placing it in the target data.

Inline XSLT is amazingly useful with BizTalk mapping, and 837 data in particular. It gives the level of control over parsing and manipulating data that is essential. The ability to look throughout the source data, regardless of where data lies in the overall hierarchy and node structure, allows for building the logic that may be required without having to build ridiculously complex functoid pattern solutions.

Service Line Mapping using Inline XSLT Call Template

In the previous example, you looked at Inline XSLT, which does not require any inputs to the Scripting functoid. Inline XSLT can parse through the source data without reference to anything. However, in some cases you may need to pass in one or more parameters. A great of example of this is in the case of Service Line mapping, which can be very involved. You may decide that the entire Service Line detail, from the TS837_2400_Loop down, is best created using XSLT. In the case at hand, the source data contains many claims, and each claim contains one or more service lines. In order to successfully map the target loop, the Transaction ID of the source claim data needs to be passed into the Inline XSLT Call Template so that only those service lines associated with the specific claim being mapped at this specific time in the map are copied over.

The code in Listing 4-3 shows a snippet of how a parameter can be passed, and how the Service Line in the target schema can be created. The TID parameter is passed in from the source. The xsl:if then checks to see if that TID matches the current data's TID (each would have a unique ID). If so, the service line gets mapped, otherwise it is ignored, as it belongs to some other claim.

Listing 4-3. Passing a Parameter into Inline XSLT Call Template Code

```
<xsl:template name="ServiceLine">
 <xsl:param name="TID" />
 <xsl:for-each select="//*[local-name()='ServiceLine']">
  <xsl:if test="../../../*/*[local-
name()='TransactionID'] = $TID">

  <xsl:element name="ns0:TS837_2400_Loop">
   <xsl:element name="ns0:LX_ServiceLineNumber">
    <LX01_AssignedNumber>
     <xsl:number /> <!-- will create numeric for this
line, ordered -->
    </LX01_AssignedNumber>
   </xsl:element>
   . . . . . . .

  </xsl:element>
  </xsl:if>
 </xsl:for-each>
</xsl:template>
```

HL Hierarchy Mapping with Functoids

Setting the HL01 and HL02 values can be a little daunting when creating an outbound 837 document from a source document that doesn't contain hierarchy relations. The best way to set your hierarchy values accurately is through the use of a Loop functoid (which you will likely have in order to loop through all of the source data to get it into the target data) and two Scripting functoid shapes. Assuming that the Loop functoid is mapped to your target TS837Q1_2000A_Loop, all HL hierarchy nodes in the target document can be set using the same two functoids. The first functoid sets the value of the HL01, and the second functoid sets the value of the HL02. Every HL01 in the target schema should have its source as the HL01 functoid, and every HL02 should have its source as the HL02 functoid. This means both of them will have many outputs. Neither has an input. Instead, the HL01 functoid declares a global variable that is available to other functoids within the map, and the HL02 functoid has access to this global variable.

The code for the HL01 functoid is shown in Listing 4-4, and the code for the HL02 functoid is shown in Listing 4-5. This code is added as Inline C# into the respective functoids. Figure 4-4 shows the functoid configuration in the map.

Listing 4-4. The HL01 Functoid

```
// global variable
int intHL01;

// this gets executed on every HL01 mapped to
public int getHL01()
{
  intHL01++;
  return intHL01;
}
```

Listing 4-5. The HL02 Functoid

```
// references global variable set and declared in HL01
script
public int getHL02()
{
  return intHL01 - 1;
}
```

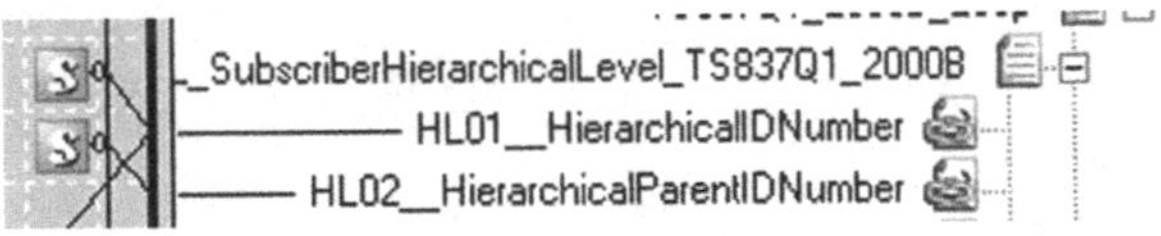

_SubscriberHierarchicalLevel_TS837Q1_2000B
———————— HL01__HierarchicalIDNumber
———————— HL02__HierarchicalParentIDNumber

Figure 4-4. Mapping HL Segments

Mapping from an Inbound 837

Mapping from an inbound 837 to a flat file or other format required by systems within your company requires some analysis. You want to ensure that your maps are as simple, efficient, and easily maintainable as possible. This may require that you use several maps to split out the mapping into logical steps, rather than trying to force everything into a single map. It may also mean you rely heavily on XSLT in the map, and don't depend too heavily on standard functoids. Given the complexity of the 837 formats, it is extremely easy to end up with a map that is completely unusable and unsupportable. What you do not want to end up with is a map that looks like that shown in Figure 4-5.

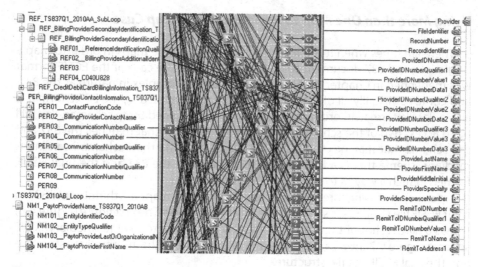

Figure 4-5. An Unsupportable and Unacceptable Mapping of Inbound 837P Data

In order to avoid ending up in a scenario like that shown in Figure 4-5, take the following steps:

- Plan your architecture - wait to start development. It is easy and tempting to just start mapping. 80% of the mapping you'll do with an inbound 837 is straightforward, and you'll find that you make quick progress with much of the implementation. Given the size of it, 80% of the mapping will be hours' worth of work. Then, as you begin on the final 20%, you'll start to run into hurdles that are very difficult to overcome, especially if you haven't built the rest of your map to support this 20%. You'll find that loops you've built and nodes you've mapped have to be rewritten to support your requirements, and the initial hours of work has now turned into days or weeks. So, in short, plan your mapping before you start development.

- Start with the most complex nodes first. Assess what the most complicated aspect of mapping is, and deal with that first. It will ensure that you are developing with the right approach, and if you find that you have to rethink your approach, you haven't wasted a lot of time on other mappings.

- Use XSLT. There are so many complexities in mapping the 837 that are reduced and simplified by using XSLT that it is a mistake not to plan on using it extensively in your maps.

The technologies used for mapping are outlined in the earlier section on outbound mapping, and are the same for inbound. Here are several examples of mapping inbound data that will be of use to you.

Using More than One Map to Handle a Single Map Case

There are times when it is critical that you use multiple maps in order to map a single inbound 837 document to an internal format. The case of the ECSIF format was mentioned in Chapter 2. This format is nearly as complex in nature as the 837, and contains virtually all of the same information. Like the 837, the ECSIF format is also a flat file format. In order to use two maps, you'll need three schemas. You will need access two of the schemas regardless: the schema that matches the 837 and the schema that matches the ECSIF flat file format. The third schema is an intermediary schema that is a halfway structure between the 837 and the final ECSIF, formed in such a way as to aid in the transformation.

An example of using three schemas and two maps for mapping the Inbound 837 to a flat ECSIF file structure is shown in the following figures. The first figure (Figure 4-6) shows a partial shot of the map from the 837P structure to the intermediary ECSIF schema. Figure 4-7 shows a shot of the mapping between the intermediary structure and the final ECSIF flat file structure.

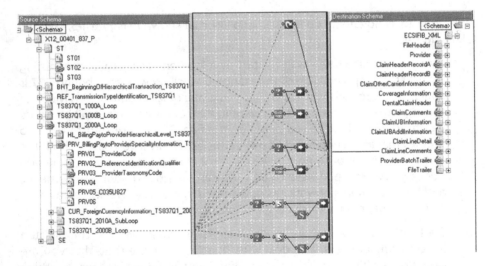

Figure 4-6. The First Map - 837P to ECSIF Intermediary

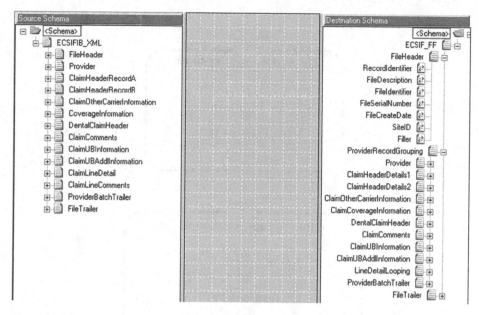

Figure 4-7. The Second Map - ECSIF Intermediary to ECSIF Flat File

When using two or more maps for a single mapping requirement, you will most likely want to incorporate an orchestration. The orchestration will allow you to stack your maps one after the other. If you were just using one map, an orchestration would not be required, as the mapping could be done directly on the ports. Figure 4-8 shows the pattern for developing an orchestration with the two maps.

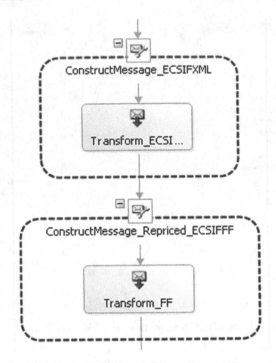

Figure 4-8. *An Orchestration with the Two Maps for ECSIF Transformation*

Using an External XSLT File for Mapping

There were two examples of using Inline XSLT earlier in this chapter, both of which could be used in conjunction with traditional mapping. There is one other type of mapping that can be used when things are simply unmanageable within a map. This option is to shell out to an external XSLT solution and skip the BizTalk mapper completely. Look at Figure 4-7 and notice that there are no mappings showing in it. This is an example of a map that uses external XSLT. In order to use external XSLT, take these steps:

- Open up a text editor and create your XSLT. An example of an XSLT file that can be used as a template in your development is shown in Listing 4-6.

■ **Note** Using an external XSLT file for mapping means that you do not have to use the BizTalk mapper interface in Visual Studio to test your maps. There are a number of free tools available on the internet that allow you to specify a source XML document to map from and an XSLT file to use in order to generate test output data.

- Create a new BizTalk map. Click anywhere on the map surface and select properties. Set the Custom XSL Path to the location of the XSLT you just created. For simplicity, add the XSLT file to the Visual Studio project at the same level as this map. The file can then be referenced as .\CustomXSLT.xslt.

Listing 4-6. Template for an External XSLT File

```
<?xml version="1.0" encoding="UTF-16"?>
<xsl:stylesheet xmlns:xsl="http://www.w3.org/1999/XSL/
Transform"
 xmlns:msxsl="urn:schemas-microsoft-com:xslt"
 xmlns:var="http://schemas.microsoft.com/BizTalk/2003/var"
 exclude-result-prefixes="msxsl var s0" version="1.0"
 xmlns:ns0="http://Company.BizTalk.Schemas.ECSIFOB_FF"
 xmlns:s0="http://Company.BizTalk.Schemas.ClaimsIB_ECSIF_XML">

<xsl:output omit-xml-declaration="yes" method="xml"
version="1.0" />
<xsl:template match="/">
 <xsl:apply-templates select="/s0:ECSIFIB_XML" />
</xsl:template>

<xsl:template match="/s0:ECSIFIB_XML">
 <ns0:ECSIF_FF>

 <!-- Your XSLT Code Goes Here -->

 </ns0:ECSIF_FF>
</xsl:template>
</xsl:stylesheet>
```

Mapping from an Inbound 834

Most of the concepts are the same between an 837 and an 834; dates have to be transformed, loops have to be structured. In this section, you'll look at mapping an 834 to a canonical structure, which is an intermediary structure that represents the internal structure of an 834. Canonical schema structures are somewhat controversial. Some organizations simply require that all inbound data that may have two or more trading partners delivering the same document types must map to a common canonical structure. Other organizations are more open to allowing for thought and good architecture to dictate when a canonical is used, and when it is not. Some of the key items to consider when deciding whether to incorporate a canonical view of the data in your BizTalk solution are described in the following sections.

Creating Global Inline C# Variables and Methods

There are frequent occasions in mapping data when there is a need to reuse a method, or to have access to a variable from multiple Scripting functoids within a map. Creating a single global inline C# Scripting functoid is an ideal way to allow for the reuse of methods and variables. The approach is simple: you can add a Scripting functoid to your map, and include the variables and methods you want to be globally accessible within it. The functoid itself should have no inputs and no outputs; it should be left orphaned somewhere on your mapping surface, and should be commented appropriately on the Label property of the functoid. An example of a functoid used for storing global methods and variables is shown in Figure 4-9, while an example of some global methods are shown in Listing 4-7.

Figure 4-9. A Scripting Functoid for Globally Accessible Variables and Methods

Listing 4-7. Globally Accessible Function Examples

```
public string GetDate()
{
  System.DateTime date = new System.DateTime();

  return date.ToString("yyyy-MM-dd");
}

public string SetGender(string gender)
{
  string result = "N/A";
  if (gender.Equals("M"))
   result = "Male";
  else if (gender.Equals("F"))
   result = "Female";

  return result;
}
```

```
public string RemoveBadChars(string input)
{
  string result = System.Text.RegularExpressions.Regex.
  Replace(input, @"[^0-9]+", string.Empty, System.Text.
  RegularExpressions.RegexOptions.None);
  return result;
}
```

> ■ **Note** A good example of needing to use a common variable is outlined in the HL mapping earlier in this chapter. Often, you will need to be able to increment a common variable from multiple locations within a map for summing and comparison purposes.

Calling Inline C# Method from within Inline XSLT

XSLT is powerful, but there are quite a few things that are challenging (or impossible) to do directly from XSLT (such as database lookups). Being able to call out to C# methods from within XSLT opens up infinite options for coding, and allows you complete freedom in how you develop your maps. In Listing 4-8, you will see a method that returns the maintenance reason based on the reason code that is passed in as a parameter. This reason code comes from the INS04_MaintenanceReasonCode element within the 834, but is passed in directly from Inline XSLT, shown in this code snippet (note the userCSharp directive):

```
<xsl:when test="current()/*[local-name()='INS_
MemberLevelDetail']/*[local-name()='INS04_
MaintenanceReasonCode']!=''">
 <xsl:element name="ns0:MaintenanceReason">
  <xsl:value-of select="userCSharp:GetMaintenanceReason
(current()/*[local-name()='INS_MemberLevelDetail']/*
[local-name()='INS04_MaintenanceReasonCode'])" />
 </xsl:element>
</xsl:when>
```

Listing 4-8. Maintenance Reason

```
public string GetMaintenanceReason(string reasonCode)
{
  string reason="";
  switch (reasonCode)
```

```
{
  case "01":reason = "Divorce"; break;
  case "02":reason = "Birth"; break;
  case "03":reason = "Death"; break;
  case "05":reason = "Adoption"; break;
  case "07":reason = "TermOfBenefits"; break;
  case "08":reason = "TermOfEmployment"; break;
  case "14":reason = "VoluntaryCancel"; break;
  case "22":reason = "PlanChange"; break;
  case "25":reason = "ChangeOfInformation"; break;
  case "28":reason = "Effectuation"; break;
  case "EC":reason = "BenefitSelection"; break;
  case "32":reason = "Marriage"; break;
  case "41":reason = "Re-enrollment"; break;
  case "43":reason = "LocationChange"; break;
  case "59":reason = "NonPayment"; break;
  case "AI":reason = "NoReason"; break;
  case "33":reason = "PersonnelData"; break;
  case "XN":reason = "NotificationOnly"; break;
  case "XT":reason = "Transfer"; break;
  default:reason = "N/A"; break;
}
return reason;
}
```

Mapping the Transaction Type for SHOP and Individual

SHOP and Individual 834 files will often be processed through the same maps. The data is almost identical between the two, and most of the code you write will be reusable between the two. In cases where you are mapping both through the same map, you'll have several code paths that must return different results depending on the type. Figure 4-10 shows the map for one example of this - mapping the transaction types - while Listing 4-8 shows the code behind the Scripting functoid.

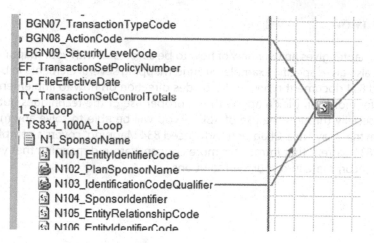

| BGN07_TransactionTypeCode
₃ BGN08_ActionCode
| BGN09_SecurityLevelCode
EF_TransactionSetPolicyNumber
TP_FileEffectiveDate
TY_TransactionSetControlTotals
1_SubLoop
| TS834_1000A_Loop
⊟ N1_SponsorName
⑤ N101_EntityIdentifierCode
⬚ N102_PlanSponsorName
⬚ N103_IdentificationCodeQualifier
⑤ N104_SponsorIdentifier
⑤ N105_EntityRelationshipCode
⑤ N106_EntityIdentifierCode

Figure 4-10. A Scripting Functoid for Mapping Transaction Type

Listing 4-8. Mapping the Transaction Type

```
public string GetTransactionType(string BGN08, string N103)
{
 string result = null;
 if (BGN08 == "2")
 {
  if (N103=="24")
   result = "SHOP Enrollment";
  else
   result = "Individual Enrollment";
 }
 if (BGN08 == "4")
 {
  if (N103=="24")
   result = "SHOP Reconciliation";
  else
   result = "Individual Reconciliation";
 }
 return result;
}
```

Conclusion

This chapter gives an overview of how to be successful with your mapping solutions. It also gives specific examples around mapping several elements in both the 837 and 834 document types, and provides direction on how to implement inline scripts for more complex maps. With the proper use of the techniques outlined – and especially through the use of XSLT – you will be able to solve any mapping problem that may arise. Chapter 9, "Advanced 834 Mapping" covers a complex outbound 834 pattern that introduces more concepts around mapping that you may want to incorporate into your own solutions.

Adapters, AS2, and Acks | Chapter 5

The actual receipt and delivery of files is central to any solution. Common approaches to receiving and sending data within the EDI space include SFTP, encrypted data over standard FTP, and secure communications over AS2. BizTalk 2013 finally introduces native SFTP support. Historically, SFTP has been handled through third-party adapters. Dealing with encrypting and decrypting data on standard ports requires custom pipeline component code. Configuring AS2 for direct party-to-party communication requires certificates and complex configurations within BizTalk. This chapter will detail the setup and configuration for each of these methods, as well as how to successfully deliver various forms of EDI acknowledgements.

SFTP

SFTP is a common option used in the exchange of data, since it ensures that the data is secure throughout the posting, storing, and retrieving stages. SFTP allows documents to be sent and received in plain text, as the protocol itself encrypts the information (with standard FTP, encrypting the file must be done through a custom pipeline component).

There are several options for sending and receiving data via SFTP in BizTalk Server. The first is the new SFTP native adapter that ships with BizTalk 2013. The second is the third-party bLogical BizTalk SFTP adapter (Blogical.Shared.Adapters.SFTP) available from CodePlex. Both of these adapters are covered here, as you may find that in some cases you may have connectivity challenges with certain SFTP servers. You will also find more robust scheduling options with the Blogical SFTP adapter.

Configuring the Native SFTP Adapter

With BizTalk 2013, the native support of SFTP is finally available. Prior to this release, only third-party (or custom) adapters could be used, but now you can set up SFTP communication as easily as standard FTP (which has been available natively since the beginning of BizTalk).

The available configurable properties on the adapter are different for inbound (receive) and outbound (send). The properties listed below come from both, and are intended to highlight the most important. Figure 5-1 shows the receive adapter properties.

> ■ **Note** Before you configure your SFTP adapter, make sure to test connectivity to the target SFTP site through a standard SFTP compatible FTP utility (one excellent option is FileZilla, which has support for a wide array of FTP and SFTP connection types). There are a number of things that may require attention before you will be able to connect successfully, and it is much easier to troubleshoot using a client utility than it is through the adapter.

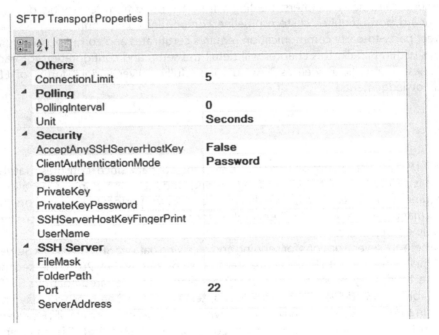

Figure 5-1. The Receive Adapter Properties

ConnectionLimit

This field sets the number of concurrent connections to the target server. By default, this is 5. If you know that the possibility exists that you could have many concurrent connections to a single SFTP server, you will need to experiment with load testing and determine how you want to configure this field. It may be best to set this to 0 (no restrictions) and let the SFTP Server manage how many connections it will allow (if it gets too many, it will throw an error back to BizTalk, and BizTalk can handle a retry of the data later).

PollingInterval and Unit

These fields are what you have available for setting a polling schedule. You can identify the polling interval. For example, if you want to check for files on the server every five minutes, you would set this the PollingInterval to 5 and the Unit to Minutes. This is pretty limited functionality, and if you need anything more robust, you will want to use the Blogical CodePlex adapter, covered later in this chapter.

AcceptAnySSHServerHostKey

This ensures that regardless of the key on the server, you will be able to make a connection. Because SFTP uses SSH, all communications require a key.

Password

Set this to the password used for connecting to the SFTP server.

FolderPath

If you are receiving data from a subdirectory of the SFTP site, you'll need to set the full path in this directory. Make sure to add a forward slash (/) before any path you enter in this property. The path is based off of the root server - so if your full path is 192.168.0.1/ChildOne/ChildTwo, you should enter /ChildOne/ChildTwo in this property, and enter 182.168.0.1 in the FolderPath property.

TargetFileName Property

The file name can be set using whatever combination of plain text and BizTalk macros that you may need. Some of the most common macros are shown in Table 5-1. Macros can be combined. If, for example, you want to show the source file name and combine it with the current datetime, you could put a value of %SourceFileName%_%datetime% in the SSH Remote File Name property.

Table 5-1. Common BizTalk Macros

Macro	Description
%datetime%	This will create a string in the format of YYY-MM-DDThhmmss based on the current UTC time of the server. If you want to take into account the local time zone, you can use %datetime.tz%
%Message_ID%	Setting your target file name with this macro included in it ensures that you will always have a uniquely named file. The Message_ID is the GUID (Globally Unique Identifier) of the message in the BizTalk Message box.
%SourceFileName%	This will be set to the value available in the FILE.ReceivedFileName of the adapter picking up the original file. In some cases, you won't have access to the source file name in your send adapter, such as when the data is originating in an orchestration. This macro retains any file extensions that may have been present (such as .pgp or .txt)

There are more macros than are shown in this table, but there are some fairly severe limitations around what you can name files. If you find that the available BizTalk macros are not flexible enough to meet your requirements, you will have to develop a custom pipeline and pipeline component to create your filename. This pipeline can be added directly to the Send Pipeline on the SFTP Send Port.

UserName

Set this to the username used for connecting to the SFTP server.

Configuring the Blogical CodePlex SFTP Adapter

This adapter is available free of charge and is very reliable. It can be downloaded, compiled, and made available within BizTalk Server within a few minutes. It has been available for a number of years, and has some capabilities (like expanded scheduling) that make it more versatile than the new native SFTP adapter.

> ■ **Note** The SFTP adapter will automatically download the original host certif-
> icate from the party you are interacting with. However, if this certificate expires
> (which is common), the SFTP adapter won't automatically be able to download
> the new certificate. If you get an exception in the Windows Event Log that says
> "HostKey does not match previously retrieved HostKey" you will need to browse
> to the `sftphostfiles.config` file and delete the HostKey setting. The di-
> rectory where this file is located will be in the Local Settings of the host user that
> the SFTP adapter runs under. For example, if your BizTalk Host instance runs under
> DOMAIN\Host_User_Account, then you will browse to `Host_User_Account\`
> `Local` Settings. The config file will be buried under a unique directory several
> levels below, so you will likely need to run a search for it once you have located
> this directory.

Once the adapter has been installed, setting it up to receive and send data
can be done by creating a new receive location or send port and setting the Type
property to SFTP (or whatever you named it during the installation). You can then
click Configure. You will want to configure the SFTP adapter with the key fields
shown in this section. In some cases, you will need to configure additional fields
beyond what is shown here, but in most cases these are all that is required.

Some of the properties listed (such as the Schedule) are unique to the receiving
of data. As you configure your SFTP send port or receive location, you'll be able to
easily identify which properties apply.

Schedule Property

This setting has some robust functionality for determining the schedule that the
source SFTP site will be queried. Clicking the ellipses on this property pops up an
interface that allows for scheduling on Daily, Weekly, Monthly, or "Timely" intervals.
You will most likely use the timely interval - every x number of minutes, for example.
In Figure 5-2, you will see the property set to poll the source SFTP site every five
minutes. In most cases, you'll be pulling your EDI data on regular intervals throughout the day, but you'll need to coordinate with your trading partner to determine if
there are any scheduling windows that should be avoided.

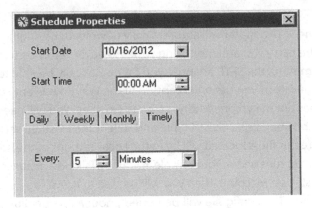

Figure 5-2. Setting the Schedule Property for "Timely" polling interval

After Get Property

This property defaults to Delete, which ensures that the file being retrieved is removed from the source SFTP site as soon as it has been successfully received by BizTalk. If there is an error in transmission, the file will remain on the server. In most cases, you will want to leave this set to Delete, but some trading partners provide archiving of data after a certain period of time, so you may want to leave the file on the server to take advantage of this. If this is not set to Delete, you will need to make sure your polling interval set in the Schedule property does not cause this same file to be retrieved multiple times before it is auto archived by the trading partner.

SSH Error Threshold Property

The SSH Error Threshold property can be used to control how many errors can be encountered before the adapter shuts down. It is fairly common to have connectivity issues with SFTP sites, and it would make sense to increase this error threshold to a sizeable amount to account for this. If left at a low number, the adapter may shut down if the source site cannot be reached over a certain period of time.

> **Note** If the SFTP adapter encounters errors, the exceptions will be logged to the Windows Event Viewer. Make sure and monitor the state of your SFTP ports, as they will automatically shut down if the error thresholds are exceeded.

SSH Host Property

This property should be set with the actual SFTP server host address. This could be an IP or a named server. It should only contain the root server name, not any subfolders. It should also not contain sftp://. An example of this property set to an IP would be 192.168.0.1.

SSH Port Property

The default port for SFTP servers is 22. If you are interacting with an SFTP server that has a different value, you will need to set the appropriate port value here.

SSH Password Property

Set this to the password used for connecting to the SFTP server.

SSH Remote Path Property

See the discussion on the FolderPath property in the section on the native SFTP adapter earlier in this chapter.

SSH Remote File Name Property

See the discussion on the TargetFileName property in the section on the native SFTP adapter earlier in this chapter.

SSH User Property

Set this to the username used for connecting to the SFTP server.

Trace Property

If you are running into exceptions when the SFTP adapter runs, you may want to set this property to True in order to log detailed information about what is happening.

Encrypted Data with Standard FTP

Using the Standard FTP adapter to send and receive data with BizTalk is a breeze - but having to deal with encrypting and decrypting data is not. This section will outline the standard properties used to configure an FTP adapter for sending or receiving data. Additionally, it will discuss some of the challenges around custom pipeline and pipeline component development, and show how to set up a custom pipeline on a Send Port and a Receive Location.

> ▇ **Note**   All data sent/received using either of the SFTP adapters is automatically encrypted.

FTP Adapter Settings

If you are sending data over FTP, you can create a Send Port in BizTalk and set the Type to FTP. If you are receiving data over FTP, you can create a BizTalk Receive Location and set the Type to FTP. In either case, you will need to set the following key properties:

- User Name - the user with which you connect to the FTP site
- Password - the password used for connections.
- Server - the FTP server. This should contain the IP or named server being connected to, and should not have the ftp:// prefix on it.
- Port - the specific port required for FTP connections
- Folder - the remote folder that you are posting data to. It should not have a leading forward slash (/) on it.
- Representation - binary or ASCII. In general, this should be set to binary, but some FTP servers don't handle binary data, so you may have to experiment with settings here.

With the FTP adapter settings configured properly, you need only to focus on the requirements of the send pipeline.

Pipelines and Pipeline Components

One of the most complex tasks in BizTalk is creating custom pipelines, as it is pure C# development. If you are using PGP for encryption and decryption, some pointers on how to develop this custom pipeline component are outlined in this section. If you need to use an alternative encryption format, then you'll need to code something specific to the tools that are used for that format. In either case, you'll need someone who is familiar with C# development to be available to work on this.

There are two items that must be set up for both the send pipeline that will encrypt data and the receive pipeline that will decrypt data. These Items are the custom pipeline and the custom pipeline component. The custom pipeline component should be developed first. Let's assume that you are going to be dealing with PGP encrypted data. There are several tools that you could use - one of the easiest to interact with is GNU Privacy Guard (www.gnupg.org). This utility allows for the generation and management of PGP keys, and provides a command line interface that can be communicated with via C# .NET code.

Calling the command line tool requires that you build out a .NET class to wrap the call so that the pipeline can pass parameters to the command line and execute it (using System.Diagnostics.ProcessStartInfo is one option to do this). Assuming you have built a wrapper class for the GNU Privacy Guard command line tool (generally located in the GNU/GnuPG/pub directory), then a sample of calling this command line tool from within a custom pipeline component to encode data is shown in Listing 5-1, while a sample of decoding data is shown in Listing 5-2.

Listing 5-1. Calling a Class to Encode Data with Parameters

```
GnuPGWrapper GPG = new GnuPGWrapper(_gnupgbindir);
GnuPGCommand GPGCommand = GPG.Command;
GPGCommand.Command = Commands.Encrypt;
GPGCommand.Recipient = _recipient;
// this is the recipient on the PGP key
GPGCommand.Passphrase = _passphrase ;
// this is the passphrase on the PGP key
GPGCommand.Armor = true;
GPGCommand.InputFile = inFile;
GPGCommand.OutputFile = outFile;
```

Listing 5-2. Calling a Class to Decode Data with Parameters

```
GnuPGWrapper GPG = new GnuPGWrapper(_gnupgbindir);
GnuPGCommand GPGCommand = GPG.Command;
GPGCommand.Command = Commands.Decrypt;
GPGCommand.InputFile = inFile;
GPGCommand.OutputFile = outFile;
GPGCommand.Passphrase = _passphrase;
// this is the passphrase of the PGP key
```

Creating the custom pipeline component will take some effort, and will depend on the encryption and decryption requirements of your solution. You will want to make a number of the fields configurable, so that you can use the send and receive pipelines on multiple trading partners. Figure 5-3 shows what these configurable properties could look like when they are set within the custom pipeline in Visual Studio.

⊟ Pipeline Component Properties	
EncryptData	True
GnuPGBinDir	C:\Program Files (x86)\GNU\GnuPG\bin
Passphrase	p@ssword1
Recipient	partnername@tradingpartner.com

Figure 5-3. Configurable Parameters on the Send Pipeline Component

The actual custom pipeline where you would be adding the custom pipeline components has to also be created. This is done within Visual Studio as a new BizTalk Pipeline project. An example of a send pipeline and what stage the custom pipeline component to encrypt should be added is shown in Figure 5-4. An example of a receive pipeline and the custom pipeline to decrypt is shown in Figure 5-5.

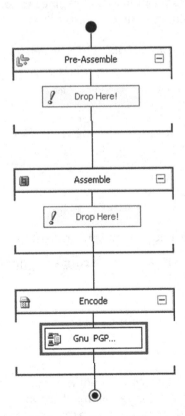

Figure 5-4. The Send Pipeline with Encrypt Component

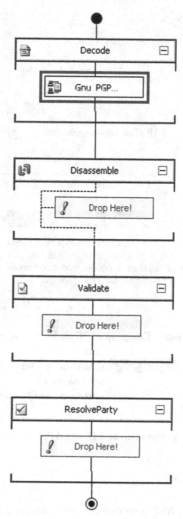

Figure 5-5. The Receive Pipeline with Decrypt Component

After you have created your pipelines and deployed them, they will be available to the Send Port and Receive Location where you have configured your FTP adapter. An example of a Receive Location with the decryption pipeline configured on it is shown in Figure 5-6.

Transport
Select a transport type and transport address below.

Type: FTP   ▼   Configure...

URI:

Send handler: BizTalkServerApplication   ▼

Send pipeline: EncryptSendPipeline   [FA.CitiBank.PGP.Pip ▼   ..

Configure Pipeline - EncryptSendPipeline   ☒

A pipeline encapsulates a set of operations that must execute in a
particular, sequential order. Pipelines often handle file coding or crypting,
as well as validation of identities. Pipelines can also contain custom
Des operations designed for particular business processes.

⊟ **Stage 1: Encode - Component: Gnu PGP encoder**

EncryptData	True
GnuPGBinDir	C:\Program Files (x86)\GNU\Gn
Passphrase	p@ssword1
Recipient	partnername@tradingpartner.coi

Figure 5-6. Configuring the pipeline on an FTP Send Port

AS2 Communications

Configuring BizTalk for AS2 communications can be a time consuming and difficult task. The most complex aspect of it is dealing with certificates. Both you and
your trading partner are required to exchange certificates and configure communications with one another with the same settings. Should your data be encrypted?
Should your MDN be signed? Do you have the correct certificate for the development environment vs. the production environment? Is your trading partner sending data in the expected format? The purpose of this section is to provide you with
enough detail around configuring and testing AS2 so that you can avoid most of
the pitfalls associated with setting this up.

Certificates

The first thing you will want to do is get your certificates set up. You'll begin by exchanging public keys with your trading partner. You should have a public and private key for your organization and a public key from the trading partner. Once you have these, you can take the following steps to set up the certificates on the BizTalk server.

CERTIFICATE CONFIGURATION FOR AS2

This exercise will demonstrate where to place and how to reference the certificates required in AS2 communications with BizTalk.

1. Log into the BizTalk server using a BizTalk service account.

2. Open the Certificate manager. From the Start Menu, click Run and type mmc. Once this is open, click File and select Add/Remove Snap-in. Select Certificates and click Add. Select the My user account option and click Finish. Select Certificates again and click Add - this time, select the Computer account option and click Next. Select the Local Computer option and click Finish. You should now have two Certificate types, as shown in Figure 5-7. Once this is complete, click OK.

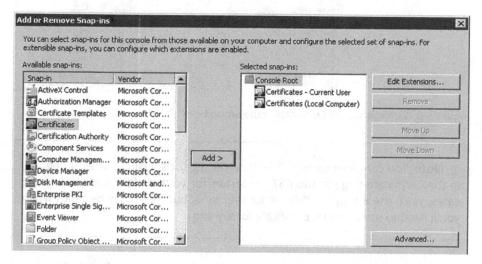

Figure 5-7. Configuring the Certificate Snap-In

3. With the Certificate console open, expand Certificates - Current User, and right click Personal. Select Import and import the private key (.pfx) for your home organization.

4. Next, expand Certificates - Local Computer, and right click Other People. Select Import and import the public key (.cer) for your trading partner's organization.

You should now see your certificates in several locations - the Personal and Other People folders of both the Local Computer and Current User. With these certificates installed, you will now be able to reference them from the appropriate locations in BizTalk.

5. In the BizTalk Administration Console, right click the BizTalk Group and select properties. Click on the Certificate option and select Browse. Your home organization's certificate should appear - select it and click OK. Figure 5-8 shows the certificate set at this level. This will be your primary certificate used to sign outbound data.

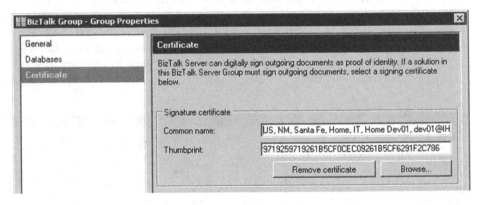

Figure 5-8. Configuring the Certificate at the Group Level

■ **Note** You can override this default certificate for specific parties, if needed, in the Certificate page of the AS2 properties for your trading partner. In most cases, you'll use a single certificate for everyone, but there may be times when you'll need to use a unique certificate for signing.

6. Right click your trading partner's BizTalk party in the BizTalk Admin Console's Parties folder and select properties. Click the Certificate option and click Browse. Select the trading partner's certificate.

There are only two other locations that you may need to configure certificates for your AS2 communications with a single trading partner - on the "Signature Certificate" page of the AS2 agreement (which allows for overriding the default home organization certificate on outbound documents and MDNs) and on any Send Ports that you may be using. However, it is unlikely that you will need to do anything with either of these, if you are engaging in standard AS2 communications.

IIS and the BizTalk HTTP Receive Location

AS2 is communication over HTTP - so setting up a site within IIS on the BizTalk Server is a requirement. There are a number of ways this can be set up, but the most common is to create a virtual directory for a specific trading partner that maps inbound requests to the BTSHTTPReceive.dll (which then pushes the inbound data to BizTalk for processing). This is a fairly involved yet easy configuration, and the following exercise outlines how to set up the various components.

> ■ **Note** In some cases, your organization may not allow companies outside your network to post data directly via HTTP to BizTalk. In this case, you'll have to set up a proxy server to allow traffic to flow through your DMZ and hit the HTTP location in BizTalk. This is a separate area of expertise from BizTalk, and should be handled by a network administrator.

CONFIGURING IIS AND THE HTTP RECEIVE LOCATION

This exercise will demonstrate how to create and configure the appropriate IIS components to handle inbound AS2 posts. It will also show how to set up the BizTalk Receive Location that receives these posts.

1. Log into the BizTalk server using a BizTalk service account.

2. Open the IIS 7 manager, click on the root server, and select the Handler Mappings option. In the Actions area on the right-hand side of the screen, click Add Script Map. Set the Request path property to BtsHttpReceive.dll and set the Executable to the location of the BtsHttpReceive.dll (this is located in the HttpReceive folder in the root BizTalk Server directory). Set the Name field to BizTalk HTTP Receive and then click the Request Restrictions button. In the Request Restrictions box, on the Access tab, select Script and click OK.

Click OK on the Add Script Map window when this has all been completed. Right click the BizTalk HTTP Receive item that was just created and select Edit Feature Permissions. In the window that opens, select the Read, Script, and Execute boxes and click OK.

See Figure 5-9 for a view of the final configuration.

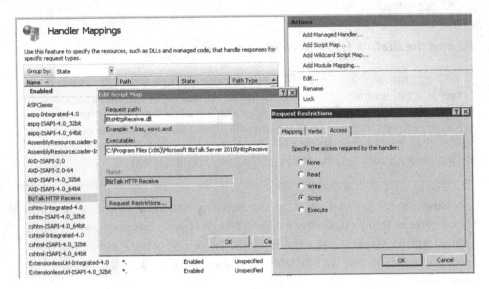

Figure 5-9. Configuring the HTTP Receive Handler Map in IIS

3. Back on the root server in IIS, click the ISAPI and CGI Restrictions icon. In the window that opens, set the BTSHTTPReceive Restriction setting to Allowed, as shown in Figure 5-10.

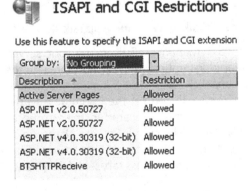

Figure 5-10. Configuring the HTTP Receive Handler Map in IIS

4. Create a new Application Pool in IIS, and set the name to BizTalkAppPool (or similar). Set the .NET Framework version property to 4.0 (whichever specific version is available to you) and the Managed Pipeline mode to Integrated.

5. Create a new virtual directory (as an Application) under the Default Web Site. The name of this site should be specific to the trading partner that you will be receiving data from over HTTP - so in this case, name it TradingPartner. Set the Application Pool to the app pool you created in the previous step and select Test Connection to ensure you are able to connect.

> **Note** Depending on your security setting, you may find that you also need to set the Physical Path Credentials to a specific account that has access to that directory. The easiest way to access this is to right click the web Application you created and select Manage Application and then Advanced Settings.

6. Click on the virtual directory you just created and select the Authentication icon. In Authentication window that opens, set Anonymous Authentication to Enabled.

This completes the setup of all IIS related components for AS2. If additional trading partners need to be set up, create one additional virtual directory for each one.

Agreements and Party Settings

In order to specify how to handle the AS2 data and how to work with the under-lying EDI document that is being sent via AS2, you will need to set up a BizTalk Party and two Agreements. One Agreement is for the AS2 messaging, and one Agreement is for dealing with the actual EDI data. The basic steps for setup are as follows for receiving AS2 data from a trading partner (sending data to a trading partner is very similar):

- Create a new BizTalk Party with the name of the trading partner you will be receiving data from.

- If you will be sending a 997/999 to the trading partner, specify the Send Port that the 997/999 will be sent out on.

- Create a new Agreement on this Party that will handle AS2 messaging (you can call it something like Agreement_AS2).
  - On the General Tab, set the Protocol property to AS2, the First Party to the trading partner and the Second Party to your home organization. Once you've set the General Tab this way, two additional tabs will appear, one for inbound data from the trading partner, and one for outbound data to the trading partner. If you are just receiving data from the trading partner and returning an MDN, you only need to configure the inbound trading partner tab.
  - On the inbound trading partner tab, on the Identifiers tab, set the AS2-From and AS2-To properties to the appropriate values as defined in your trading partner agreement. These must match what is on the AS2 envelope being sent to you. Figure 5-11 shows an example of these settings.

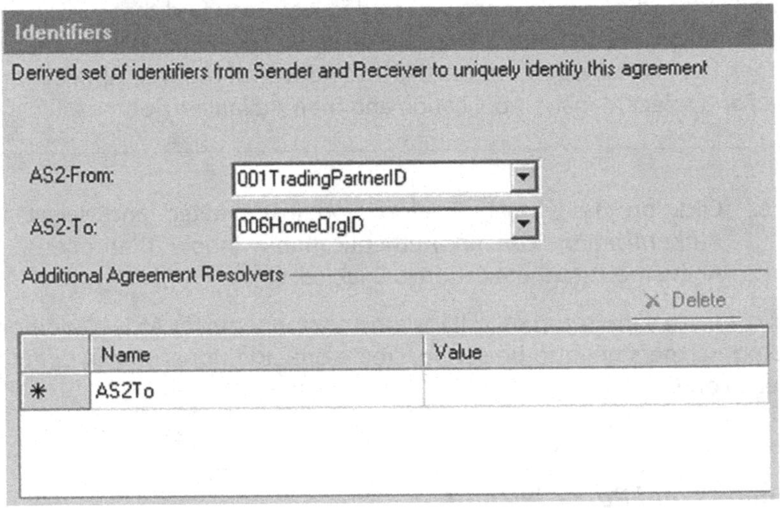

Figure 5-11. The Identifiers tab in the AS2 Agreement

  - On the Validation tab for the AS2 Agreement, you can set the appropriate values for validation of the data. For example, if you are receiving a signed and encrypted inbound post from a trading partner, then you would set the properties as shown in Figure 5-12.

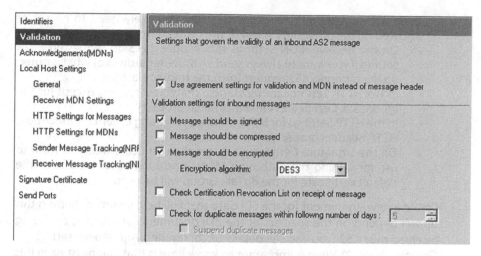

Figure 5-12. The Validation tab in the AS2 Agreement

◦ On the Acknowledgement tab of the AS2 Agreement, you can set the properties that pertain to the MDN response back to the trading partner. If you need to send an unsigned MDN, you can use the properties as shown in Figure 5-13. If you are sending a signed MDN, then the certificate specific in the Signature Certificate settings will be used (or, if none is specified, then the default certificate associated with the BizTalk Group will be used).

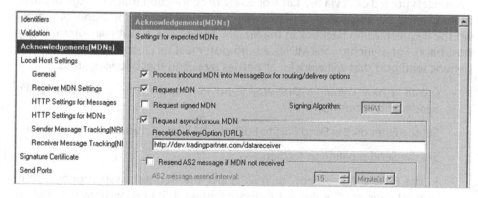

Figure 5-13. The Acknowledgement tab in the AS2 Agreement

- ° There are some additional properties that will likely need to be set or adjusted on the other tabs. A few of the most common are noted here.
  - On the Receive MDN Settings tab, enable the Sign requested MDN setting if you want to always send an MDN, regardless of what is noted on the inbound AS2 request from the trading partner.
  - In the HTTP Settings for Messages, enable everything except for the Ignore SSL Certificate Name mismatch property.
  - In the HTTP Settings for MDN, enable everything except for the Unfold HTTP headers property.
  - On the Signature Certificate tab, set the certificate that you want to use for signing the outbound MDN. If nothing is selected here, the default certificate for the BizTalk Group will be used.

- Create a new Agreement for the EDI data that will be consumed. Setting this up will depend on the specifics of the EDI document type(s) that are being received over AS2 (you can see details of configuring Agreement settings in Chapters 2 and 3). What is important to know here is that you must have this additional Agreement in place so that BizTalk knows how to process the EDI data once the AS2 Agreement has successfully completed the data transfer.

The Generic MDN Send Port for Asynchronous Messages

The MDN is the acknowledgement for AS2 posts. There are two possible methods for postback of an MDN - synchronous and asynchronous. The synchronous response is posted back via the same open HTTP connection that the original document came in on, and does not require any additional BizTalk components (simply set the Request MDN checkbox in the BizTalk Agreement, and it will automatically post back). For asynchronous MDNs, a send port must be created. You can create a generic send port that will work for all parties by taking the following steps:

- Create a new Dynamic One-way Send Port and name it something like SendAsyncronousMDNs

- Set the Filter on the Send Port to EdiIntAS.IsAS2AsynchronousMdn == True

- Set the Send pipeline to AS2Send

- In the BizTalk Agreement for AS2, select the Request asynchronous MDN property and set the Receipt-Delivery-Option (URL) property to the URL on which the trading partner is expecting data to be delivered.

When the configuration is set like this, the moment a document is received from a trading partner, BizTalk will automatically create an MDN and drop it on the BizTalk Message Box. The SendAsynchronousMDNs send port will subscribe to this document and send it out to the URL specified in the Receipt-Deliver-Option (URL) property on whatever trading partner's Agreement was just used to receive the data.

Testing your AS2 Configuration

One of the most challenging (and frustrating) aspects of AS2 configuration is the actual trading partner testing. The best advice is to plan to set up your AS2 configuration in stages. Try to exchange plain text data (unencrypted and unsigned) first before dealing with the various settings requiring certificates. If you can get the plain, un-encoded data to flow (and the MDN to return) successfully, then you can move into testing encryption and signing.

There are many things that can go wrong during testing, and the error messages are often very generic and cryptic. The errors could be on your side, or they could be on the trading partner's side. The more you can do to limit what is being tested at any given stage, the quicker you will be able to get to resolution and completion.

Sending 997/999 Acknowledgements

There are several types of acknowledgements that can be sent in response to EDI communications - Functional (997/999), Technical (TA), and MDNs (for AS2). Configuring and sending MDN acknowledgements was covered earlier in the AS2 section in this chapter. Technical Acknowledgements are rarely required, and are identical in setup to the Functional. You will now look at sending the Functional acknowledgements for the EDI data itself. The steps to take are as follows:

- Open the BizTalk Party Agreement that relates to the documents and trading partner that you need to set up the Functional Acknowledgement for, click on the Acknowledgements tab. You will be able to set a checkbox next to 997 Expected, as shown in Figure 5-14.

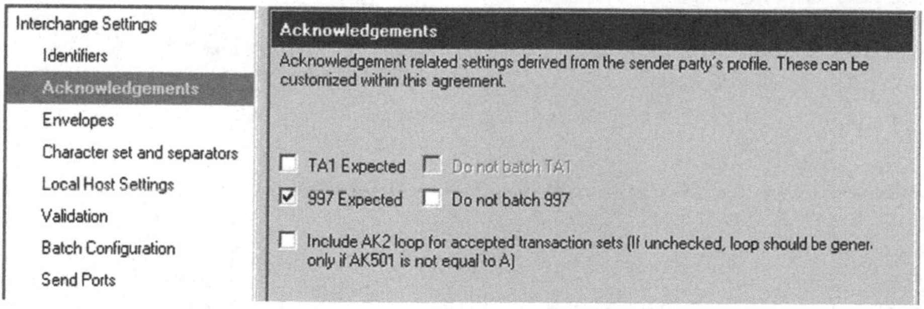

Figure 5-14. The Acknowledgement tab in the EDI Agreement

- Set up one Send Port per trading partner. These send ports will subscribe directly to the BizTalk Message Box, and will filter on the specific trading partner required. The Send Port should have the following settings:
  - ○ The transport type - FTP, SFTP, or other. Set the appropriate connection information for the actual adapter that will be used to connect to the trading partner.
  - ○ The Send Pipeline should be set to EdiSend - or, if you are required to encrypt 997 data (which is uncommon), you will need to add your custom send pipeline to do the encryption.
  - ○ Three filters, as follows:
    - EDI.IsSystemGeneratedAck == true
    - EDI.ST01 == 997 (or 999 if version 5010)
    - EDI.ISA06 == [this should be the specific trading partner's ID that you are configuring for this specific Send Port - this ID can be retrieved from the Party settings of the BizTalk Agreement where you have configured 997s to be sent]
- Depending on your configuration, you may need to associated the 997/999 Send Port with your Agreement on the Send Ports tab.

Once you have these settings configured, BizTalk will automatically generate a 997/999 when the inbound EDI document is received and drop it on the BizTalk Message Box. Next, the Send Port will pick it up and deliver it to the specified destination.

Conclusion

This chapter has gone in depth on the most common transport mechanisms for any BizTalk EDI health care implementation you may need to build out. It has also shown how to deal with acknowledgements - 997/999s and MDNs. With the information related to AS2, SFTP, and encrypted data over FTP that has been covered, you'll be able to successfully develop and interact with trading partners.

Solution: Receiving 834 Data

There are two high-level inbound architectures for the 834. The first is a simple model where the 834 EDI arrives, is picked up by BizTalk, and mapped to an internal data structure. This simple model can have any variety of components and additional steps (business rules, orchestrations, etc.), but the basic flow is simple - especially when compared to the common alternative. The alternative, second model, is more complex, where the 834 is received, archived, and split into its individual parts (usually based on subscriber and dependent information). All of the split data runs in parallel, with each one instantiating its own mapping, orchestrations, and other processes. Additionally, recording of basic metrics across all of the data for reporting is required. This chapter will walk through the specifics of this more involved advanced processing of the 834 data.

The solution described uses only a single schema (the 834 XSD), and relies heavily on pipeline components to do most of the processing. Other chapters in this book outline how to use multiple schemas and maps to achieve the necessary results. The intention of this chapter is to give an overview of something that is more code-centric and doesn't rely on the traditional aspects of BizTalk development (and also matches some very common requirements in the processing of inbound 834 development).

Figure 6-1 shows an overview of the solution that will be presented in this chapter. Portions of this solution are further explained in other chapters, as noted throughout the text.

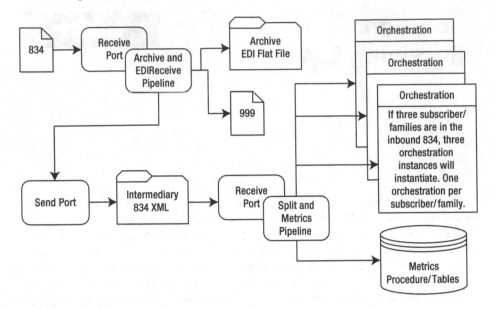

Figure 6-1. Inbound 834 Solution Overview

> ■ **Note** The remaining discussions in this chapter assume that you have read through Chapters 2, 3, and 5, all of which provide best practice recommendations and additional details about most of these topics. Chapters 7 and 8 build out the components of certain aspects presented in this chapter.

Visual Studio Solution

For this solution, the following Visual Studio projects and namespaces will be used:

- Solution Name: Company.BizTalk. You can add the projects in this chapter to the solution that was created in earlier chapters. In some cases, you may want to break your code into separate solutions, but most likely you will want to limit this to a solution for inbound EDI projects and a solution for outbound EDI projects. There is a lot of potential for reuse of components (such as helper libraries and schemas) across projects, and it is often very useful to have everything related in a single solution for reference purposes.

- Schema. There is one schema that will be used in this solution - the 834 5010 schema that ships with BizTalk. The solution presented will not use BizTalk for mapping to any other format. The schema will be contained in its own project named Company.BizTalk.Schemas.EDI.

- Helper Library. There will be one external .NET assembly project with the namespace of Company.BizTalk.Utility.

- Orchestration. There will be one orchestration used, which will be in its own project called Company.BizTalk.Process.InboundX834.

- Pipeline. There is one pipeline project with two pipelines in it. The project name is Company.BizTalk.Pipelines.Split834.

- Pipeline Components. There are several pipeline components that will be created, one for archiving from the first receive location and one for handling metrics. These projects are called Company.BizTalk.PipelineComponents. Split834 and Company.BizTalk.PipelineComponents.EDI.Archival.

The Schema Project

There will be one schema required for this project - the 834 5010 schema that ships with BizTalk. You should be able to use a single 834 schema for all of your trading partners, even if some of them have different validation requirements. The way to think of your schema is that it is your internal representation of your 834 data - just like if you had a SQL database structure that was a common way to store information. You shouldn't try to create a schema for each trading partner - a map per trading partner is essential, but a single 834 for all trading partners is also critical (though in some rare instances you may find that you do need a separate 834 schema for a rogue trading partner that does not utilize the 834 properly).

In this solution, the 834 schema will be used on the initial receive port/location. After this initial validation of the schema occurs, the data will be treated as generic XML throughout the rest of the process (most notably in the orchestration).

Take the following steps to create a project that has the correct 834 BizTalk schema for your implementation:

- Create a new project in Visual Studio called Company.BizTalk.Schemas.EDI.

- Find the HIPPA folder in the BizTalk EDI schema collection (the zip file containing all of the schemas is MicrosoftEdiXSDTemplates.exe, located in the XSD_Schema folder in the root BizTalk install directory). There are several versions available - 4010 and 5010 (along with an Errata folder that addresses some schema inconsistencies). You'll use the 5010 for this chapter. Click on the 834 folder and notice there is a "single" and a "multiple" available for selection. The schema you will need to use will depend on your batching requirements (if you have any).

- For a detailed discussion about batching, look at Chapter 3 "Solution: Sending 837P Data."

> ■ **Note** Inbound 834 data can be split at several levels using the XSD and no other code. The solution in this chapter shows how to split the document using a pipeline component, for some very specific processing requirements, but the data can be split using the schema as discussed at `http://msdn.microsoft.com/en-us/library/bb226327.aspx`

The .NET Helper Library Project

As other solutions in this book have done, the current inbound 834 solution will utilize a .NET helper library for some of the work that is being done. Much of the code in this library could be included directly in the pipeline component code that you will be looking at shortly, but because the orchestration requires some interaction with the database (and therefore uses a .NET helper library), centralizing some of the tasks in a utility class library makes more organizational sense. You are free to structure this however you would like, but using a standard pattern that includes a helper/utility assembly is a good habit to acquire.

> ■ **Note** Remember to mark your .NET classes as Serializable (by typing [Serializable] directly above the class declaration) as mentioned in Chapter 2 "Solution: Receiving 837P Data."

One of the methods in the helper library is the code that is used to make the connection to Oracle and execute the procedure that returns the historic XML. The code for this is shown in Listing 6-1. Another method that would be included in this is the method used to execute the SQL Server stored procedure that runs the business rules - this code is shown in detail in Chapter 8 "Custom Business Rules".

Listing 6-1. Retrieve Historic XML Data from Oracle

```
public void RetrieveHistoricalXML(string
connectionString,string subscriber,
 out string historicXML, out string errorDesc)
{
 OracleConnection oConnection = new OracleConnection
(connectionString);
 oConnection.Open();
```

```
string sproc = "TARGET.PKG_XMLRESULTSETS.
RetrieveHistoric";
OracleCommand oCmd = new OracleCommand(sproc,
oConnection);

oCmd.CommandText = sproc;
oCmd.CommandType = System.Data.CommandType.
StoredProcedure;

OracleParameter paramSubscriberNum = new
OracleParameter("in_Subscriber",
  OracleDbType.Varchar2, 200);
paramSubscriberNum.Direction = System.Data.
ParameterDirection.Input;
paramSubscriberNum.Value = subscriber;
oCmd.Parameters.Add(paramSubscriberNum);

OracleParameter paramXMLarameterName = new
OracleParameter("out_XML", OracleDbType.XmlType);
paramXMLarameterName.Direction = System.Data.
ParameterDirection.Output;
oCmd.Parameters.Add(paramXMLarameterName);

OracleParameter paramErrorMessage = new
OracleParameter("out_errorMessage",
  OracleDbType.Varchar2, 200);
paramErrorMessage.Direction = System.Data.
ParameterDirection.Output;
oCmd.Parameters.Add(paramErrorMessage);

oCmd.ExecuteNonQuery();

historicXML = ((Oracle.DataAccess.Types.OracleXmlType)
(paramXMLarameterName.Value)).Value.ToString();

errorDesc = paramErrorMessage.Value.ToString();

oConnection.Close();
oConnection.Dispose();
}
```

> ■ **Note**   In order to call Oracle, you will need to have the Oracle client tools installed on your development machine, and also on your BizTalk instance. You will need to reference Oracle.DataAccess.dll in your Visual Studio project.

The Orchestration Project

The inbound 834 EDI instance is split into individual instances, based on the number of subscribers. If there are 100 subscribers, then there will be 100 individual orchestration instances that will instantiate. This allows for highly efficient utilization of the BizTalk and SQL core resources (CPU, RAM, threads, etc.) and ensures that large batches of inbound data can be handled. It also ensures that in the event of an error in processing one subscriber's data, the rest of the inbound data is not delayed (why stop the processing of 99 good records if only one has data issues?). It is common in 834 files (especially month-end reconciliation files) to have tens (or hundreds) of thousands of records in a single file - so the splitting of data is essential for performance. It also eliminates all looping and other similar structures from the orchestration, which keeps things simple and easy to maintain.

The orchestration for this solution picks up the split 834 and then takes two steps - the first step is to lookup the historical information in the internal database (in this case, Oracle), and the second step is to call a custom business rules stored procedure. The data returned from the call to Oracle is in XML, and the two parameters passed to the business rules stored procedure are also XML.

> ■ **Note**   Refer to Chapter 8 for details around the implementation of the calls shown in the orchestration in Figure 6-2.

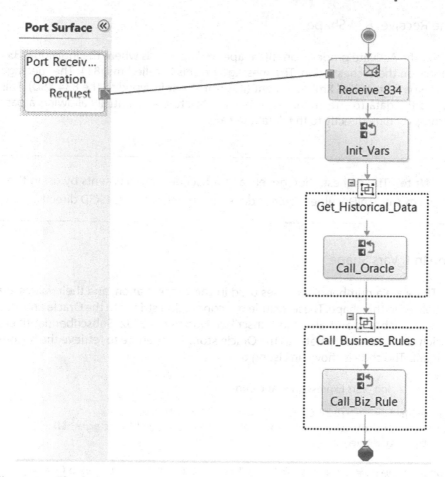

Figure 6-2. The Orchestration

Details behind each of the shapes in this orchestration are given below, to show how the code is referenced and how the various database procedures are called. Notice that there are no adapters used for interacting with the database. The more you can move to eliminate the use of adapters (especially for database interactions) the easier your solutions will become to develop, maintain, test, troubleshoot, and deploy. Making intelligent decisions about how best to utilize the technology available to you is critical to becoming an expert BizTalk developer, and you should find that abandoning the use of most of the adapters (WCF, SQL, etc.) will lead to better solutions.

The Receive_834 Shape

Set the Activate property on this shape to True. This is where the individual 834 arrives on the orchestration. The message on this is called msg834. The message is of type System.Xml.XmlDocument (it is not strongly typed to the 834 XSD). This allows the data to stream in, regardless of structure - essentially allowing a pass through of data directly to the database calls.

> ■ **Note**   The orchestration generically subscribes to documents by using the System.Xml.XmlDocument type. It does not reference the 834 XSD directly.

The Init_Vars Shape

There are a number of variables used in this orchestration, and their values are initialized in this shape. These include the connection strings to the Oracle and SQL Server databases and also the Subscriber Number (REF02_SubscriberIdentifier), which is used as a parameter to the Oracle stored procedure to retrieve the historical XML. The code is shown in Listing 6-2.

Listing 6-2. Init_Vars Expression Shape Code

```
fileName = msg834(FILE.ReceivedFileName);
System.Diagnostics.EventLog.WriteEntry("Message ID:
",strFileName);

subscriber = xpath(msg834,"string(//*[local-name()=
'REF02_SubscriberIdentifier']/text())");
System.Diagnostics.EventLog.WriteEntry("Subscriber:
",strSubscriberNumber);

oracleConnectionString = System.Configuration.
ConfigurationSettings.AppSettings["Company.
BizTalk.X834.ConnectionString.Oracle"];
```

> ■ **Note**   Adding simple logging statements in the orchestration Expression shapes can aid debugging, and are easy to add. Listing 6-2 shows several examples of this easy approach. It should only be used for development, and the code should be removed prior to deployment to production.

> ▪ **Note** See Chapter 2 "Solution: Receiving 837P Data" for details about how to read from the BizTalk configuration file.

The Call_Oracle Shape

This shape calls Oracle using the code shown earlier in this chapter in the .NET helper assembly. The Expression shape code simply passes parameters into this method, as shown in Listing 6-3, and gets back a string containing the XML returned directly from the stored procedure.

Listing 6-3. Calling the .NET Assembly Method to Read from Oracle

```
//Get Historical XML result set from Oracle
objDataAccess.RetrieveHistoricalXML(sqlConnectionString,
subscriber
,out historical, out errorDesc);
```

The Call_Biz_Rule Shape

This shape calls a SQL Server stored procedure, which is shown in detail, along with all of the other related components, in Chapter 8. This Expression shape code (shown in Listing 6-4) constructs the two XML documents - the historical XML from the call to the Oracle database, and the current 834 XML, which instantiated the orchestration - and passes them into the stored procedure via the C# method (also shown in Chapter 8).

Listing 6-4. Calling the .NET Assembly Method to Call the SQL Stored Procedure

```
// load the inbound 834 message into a variable of type XML
xml834 = new System.Xml.XmlDocument();
xml834 = msg834;

// the connection string is set in the C# code that is
being called, so no need
// to pass a connection string like you did with the
Oracle process above
// the "historical" parameter was set in the call to
Oracle, and contains the
// XML string
objDataAccess.callBusinessRules(historical,
xml834.InnerXML, out errorDesc);
```

The Pipeline and Pipeline Component Projects

This solution heavily utilizes custom pipelines and pipeline components, and a full chapter (Chapter 7 "Pipelines for 834 Processing") is devoted to outlining how these BizTalk artifacts are built and incorporated into the solution. The key item to point out here is that due to the way pipelines stread data, and the way the existing EDIReceive pipeline processes data, you may find that you have to split your work into multiple pipelines which are added to different receive locations. The solution described in this chapter does the following:

- Uses two receive ports and two receive locations.

- On the first port/location, the standard EDIReceive pipeline is used (this can be combined with the archiving of the data in a custom pipeline).

> ■ **Note** The EDIReceive pipeline will handle party resolution, EDI schema validation, and generation of the acknowledgement (997/999). The acknowledgement, if generated, will need to be routed from the MessageBox back to the trading partner using a send port (or orchestration, if advanced processing is required). See Chapter 5 "Adapters, AS2 and Acks" for details about handling acknowledgements.

- On the second pipeline, the splitting of the inbound EDI 834 occurs. This is also where metrics can be applied. The reason that there are two pipelines required is that the data in this pipeline needs to be in XML, which is not available until after the standard EDIReceive pipeline triggers in the first pipeline.

Refer to Chapter 7 for all of the details around creating the custom pipelines and pipeline components used in this solution.

Setting up the BizTalk Components

Chapter 2 details all of the remaining steps you will need to work through in order to deploy your solution, configure the various BizTalk artifacts (like receive ports and locations), and set the appropriate values in the party settings and agreements. If you have configured your 837 solutions, you should be able to piggy back off of what you already have in order to have the current 834 solution execute. At a high level, the following steps will need to be taken:

- Deploy the various assemblies to BizTalk and the GAC.

- Create the appropriate ports and receive locations, as shown in the diagram from Figure 6-1.
  - ° The first receive port/location combo get the EDI document. You can use the default EDIReceive pipeline on your receive location. If you want to include archiving of the original data, then you would need to add the custom pipeline/pipeline component to this location.
  - ° The send port subscribes directly to the receive port you created in the previous bullet, and simply writes the XML out to a temporary "staging" file directory.
  - ° The second receive port/location pick up the EDI 834 XML produced by the send port. This uses the custom pipeline and pipeline component that you created for this project (outlined in full in Chapter 7).

- Modify the existing party agreement that you set up for the 837 (again, see Chapter 2) to allow for the receiving of 834 data. The only thing that you should have to do for this is to add in the appropriate 834 detail on the Validation and Envelopes tabs in the agreement settings.

- Start the receive locations, and bind and enable the orchestration.

- Copy the pipeline component assembly/assemblies to the Pipeline Components directory in the root BizTalk installation folder.

- Add all appropriate configurable values to the BizTalk configuration file.

- Restart the BizTalk host instance to ensure all of these changes take effect.

Conclusion

Handling inbound 834 EDI data often requires more involved coding and architecture than other document types. While every solution varies, the purpose of the discussions in this chapter were to broaden your understanding of options available to you in processing inbound data, and to detail specifics about dealing with the 834 information itself. Chapters 7 and 8 build on the concepts outlined in this chapter, and provide in-depth information on how to build your advanced 834 solution. For those of you who have simple requirements around the 834, don't let the discussions in this chapter sway you - keep things as simple as possible, and only incorporate these additional pieces of architecture if you absolutely require them. If you can get away with not writing a custom pipeline component, then by all means do so!

Pipelines for 834 Processing

In the previous chapter, you looked at receiving an inbound 834 document. In the process described, there were two key areas of functionality that were handled in custom pipeline/pipeline components. The functionality and development of these components are covered in this chapter. Archiving the data, along with EDI validation and disassembly will be covered first (as these map to the first stage of work outlined in Chapter 6 "Solution: Receiving 834 Data." Splitting and building the metrics will be handled second in this discussion.

> ■ **Note** There are several ways to handle what is presented in this chapter. The components presented here will work in a production environment, and are solid architecturally.

Pipelines

The naming and structure of the pipeline project was outlined in Chapter 6. There are two pipelines stored in a single project. The project name for this solution is Company.BizTalk.Pipelines.Split834. The pipeline components are split into two projects. Company.BizTalk.PipelineComponents.Split834 and Company.BizTalk. PipelineComponents.EDI.Archive.

Archiving and EDI Validation/Disassembly

The first pipeline – which handles the archiving and EDI specific portions of the processing – is call EDIArchive.btp, and is shown in Figure 7-1. In the Decode stage of this first pipeline, a custom pipeline component has been added (see Listing 7-1 for specifics on this component's code). In the Disassemble stage, the standard EDI disassembler pipeline component has been added (this is available in the Toolbox, as shown in Figure 7-2).

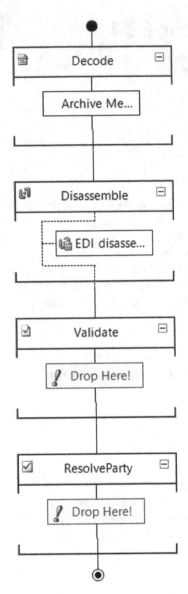

Figure 7-1. The EDIArchive Pipeline

Listing 7-1. Writing the Archive Data in the StreamOnReadEvent Method

```
// the trading partner ID, used for dynamic looking in
the config file, is
// pulled from the original streamed message using a
simple substring lookup.
// This is the location in the actual EDI 834 text string
string ID = original834String.Substring(35, 15).Trim();
string dir = System.Configuration.ConfigurationManager.
AppSettings[ID];

// the dir path needs to be extended with the file naming
pattern you want for // archived data.  This can be
something as simple as [ID]_[GUID].txt.

using (
 FileStream FAS = new FileStream(dir, FileMode.Append,
 FileAccess.Write))
 {
  using (BinaryWriter FBWriter = new BinaryWriter(FAS)
  {
  FBW.Write(rargs.buffer, 0, rargs.bytesRead);
  FBW.Flush();
  FBW.Close();
  }
 }
```

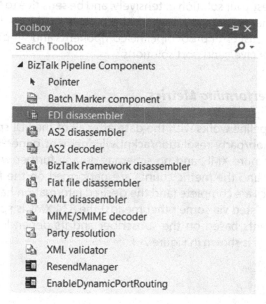

Figure 7-2. EDI Disassembler is Available in the Pipeline Component Toolbox

The archiving of the data takes the exact EDI 834 message that arrived and writes it to a specified file directory in its native EDI format prior to being validated and disassembled in the EDI disassembler component. Chapter 2 showed how to do this from an orchestration Expression shape through a C# method in the helper library. The approach in the pipeline component is similar – grab the stream of data, determine the target archive directory and file name (which is configurable, based on the trading partner), and write it out.

■ **Note** Building a pipeline component from scratch can be a daunting task. Thankfully, there are several third-party tools available that help with this development. One of the most valuable is a project on CodePlex which creates the majority of the core pipeline component code for you (it is available for download at `http://btsplcw.codeplex.com`).

The core piece of custom functionality in the archive process is the writing of the data to a target directory without impacting the message stream prior to the EDI disassembly and validation. Listing 7-1 shows code that can be used to write the data within the StreamOnReadEvent method of the pipeline component. This is a fairly common approach to archiving data in a pipeline component, and has some limitations. If the data reading terminates mid process (such as in a server reboot scenario) it is possible that only a portion of the message will be archived. You will want to test your solution extensively, and be sensitive to the requirements of your environment. There are several alternatives to this archiving approach, including more robust error proof pipeline components and simple processes such as multiple hop receive/send port solutions.

Splitting and Performing Metrics

The second pipeline works with the data after all of the EDI specific tasks have occurred (validation/party resolution/acknowledgement generation/etc.). At this point, the data is pure XML, and no schemas do any further work. The pipeline receives the data and the metric counts are performed on the full EDI 834 XML. Once these metrics are complete (and the desired information has been written to a database or persisted via some other means) the 834 XML is split into individual 834 XML documents based on the subscriber and its dependents. The pipeline (called Split834.btp is shown in Figure 7-3.

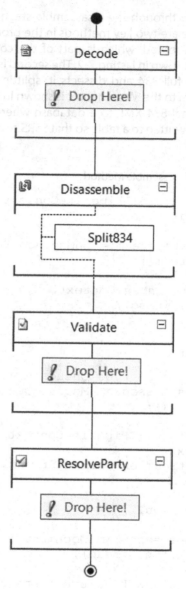

Figure 7-3. The Split834 Pipeline

The 834 XML is passed through the disassemble stage where the data can be parsed and split up. There are two key methods in the processing of this data. The first is the Disassemble method, which is part of the core pipeline component framework, and which is shown in Listing 7-2. The second is Create834, the method that parses through the full 834 and dissects it, splitting it into individual 834 messages and sends them to the MessageBox, is shown in Listing 7-3. This method also passes off the original 834 XML to a database where the metric counts are performed (and the data written to a table so that SSRS or other similar process can report on the information).

Listing 7-2. A Customized Disassemble Method

```
public void Disassemble(IPipelineContext context,
IBaseMessage inMsg)
{
 Stream originalDataStream = inMsg.BodyPart.
GetOriginalDataStream();

 Create834(context, inMsg.Context,
originalDataStream,inMsg);
}
```

Listing 7-3. The 834 Splitter

```
// declare an object of type Queue
private Queue<IBaseMessage> _MessageQueue = new
Queue<IBaseMessage>();

private void Create834(IPipelineContext context,
IBaseMessageContext
 sourceContext, Stream enrollmentStream, IBaseMessage
inMsg)
{
 IBaseMessage msg = null;

 XmlDocument xmlDoc = new XmlDocument();
 xmlDoc.Load(enrollmentStream);

 // take the full 834 XML document and send it to a
stored procedure
 // for processing the metrics.  See Listing 7-4 for
sample SQL for these
 // metrics.  There are several samples throughout this
book on C# code that
 // can be used to call a stored procedure.
 [... call metrics SQL ...]
```

```
string XML = xmlDoc.InnerXml;
string path = null;

XPathNavigator navigator = xmlDoc.CreateNavigator();

XPathNodeIterator xi = navigator.Select(@"/*[local-
  name()='X12_00501_834']/*[local-name()='TS834_2000_
Loop']/*[local-
  name()='INS_MemberLevelDetail'][INS01_
MemberIndicator[.='Y']]");
XPathNavigator top, toptMiddle, endMiddle, end;
string messageType =
  "http://schemas.microsoft.com/BizTalk/EDI/X12/2006/
X12_00501_834";
string systemNamespace = "http://schemas.microsoft.com/
BizTalk/2003/system-properties";

while (xi.MoveNext())
{
 var xmlDocSplit = new XmlDocument();
 enrollmentStream.Position = 0;
 xmlDocSplit.Load(enrollmentStream);
 XPathNavigator navSplit = xmlDocSplit.CreateNavigator();

 top = toptMiddle = endMiddle = end = null;

 //Go previous
 if (xi.CurrentPosition > 1)
 {
  // 2000 Loop
  path = @"/*[local-name()='X12_00501_834']/*[local-
   name()='TS834_2000_Loop'][1]";
  top = navSplit.SelectSingleNode(path);
  //last 2000
  path = String.Format(@"(/*[local-
name()='X12_00501_834']/*[local-
   name()='TS834_2000_Loop']/*[local-name()='INS_
MemberLevelDetail']
   [INS01_MemberIndicator[.='Y']]/parent::node())[{0}]/
preceding-
   sibling::*[1]", xi.CurrentPosition.ToString());
  toptMiddle = navSplit.SelectSingleNode(path);
 }

 //Go next
 if (xi.CurrentPosition < xi.Count)
```

```
  {
   //first 2000
   path = String.Format(@"(/*[local-
name()='X12_00501_834']/*[local-
    name()='TS834_2000_Loop']/*[local-name()='INS_
MemberLevelDetail']
    [INS01_MemberIndicator[.='Y']]/parent::node())[{0}]",
(xi.CurrentPosition +
    1).ToString());
   endMiddle = navSplit.SelectSingleNode(path);
   //last 2000
   path = "/*[local-name()='X12_00501_834']/*[local-
    name()='TS834_2000_Loop'][position()=last()]";
   end = navSplit.SelectSingleNode(path);
  }

  if (top != null)
  {
   navSplit.MoveTo(top);
   navSplit.DeleteRange(toptMiddle);
  }
  if (endMiddle != null)
  {
   navSplit.MoveTo(endMiddle);
   navSplit.DeleteRange(end);
  }

  msg = context.GetMessageFactory().CreateMessage();
  msg.AddPart("Body", context.GetMessageFactory().
CreateMessagePart(), true);
  msg.BodyPart.Data = new
   MemoryStream(UTF8Encoding.UTF8.GetBytes(xmlDocSplit.
OuterXml));

  //Copy properties from the original
  msg.Context = sourceContext;
  msg.Context.Promote("MessageType", systemNamespace,
messageType);

  // queue the split message for processing
  _MessageQueue.Enqueue(msg);
  }
}
```

> ■ **Note** As mentioned in Chapter 6, inbound 834 data can be split at several levels using the XSD and no other code. The solution in this chapter shows how to split the document using a pipeline component, for some very specific processing requirements, but the data can be split using the schema as discussed at `http://msdn.microsoft.com/en-us/library/bb226327.aspx`.

SQL Code for Metrics

The metrics that have been referred to in this case include coming up with several counts on the full 834 XML file. These counts include total number of member records, total number of groups, and total number of subscribers. Taking the full XML and passing it to a stored procedure allows for the use of simple XQuery statements that can be used in conjunction with temporary tables to insert data directly into the target tables. Alternatively, C# could be used to do the metrics if you do not have any need to write the data out to a SQL table for reporting. Listing 7-4 gives an example of code to get the mentioned metrics from an 834 XML file.

Listing 7-3. The 834 Splitter

```
CREATE PROCEDURE [dbo].[GetMetrics]
 @XML as nvarchar(max)
AS
BEGIN
SET NOCOUNT ON;

-- replace all ns0: declarations for ease of XQuery
queries
SELECT CAST(REPLACE(@XML,'ns0:','')as XML)as sourceXML
INTO #TempXML
DECLARE @totalMemberRecords as int
        ,@totalSubscriberRecords as int
        ,@totalGroups as int

-- get a count of distinct groups in the 834
SET @totalGroups =
(
 SELECT
 COUNT(distinct substring(h.value('REF_SubLoop[1]/REF_
MemberPolicyNumber[1]
  /REF02_MemberGrouporPolicyNumber[1]','varchar
(max)'),3,4)) as [Group]
 FROM #TempXML
```

```
CROSS APPLY sourceXML.nodes('//X12_00501_834/TS834_2000_
Loop')as header(h)
)

SET @totalMemberRecords =
(
 SELECT COUNT(h.value('INS_MemberLevelDetail[1]/INS01_
MemberIndicator[1]'
  ,'varchar(max)'))
 FROM #TempXML
 CROSS APPLY sourceXML.nodes('//X12_00501_834/TS834_2000_
Loop')as header(h)
)

SET @totalSubscribers =
(
 SELECT COUNT(h.value('INS_MemberLevelDetail[1]/INS01_
MemberIndicator[1]'
 ,'varchar(max)'))
 FROM #TempXML
 CROSS APPLY sourceXML.nodes('//X12_00501_834/TS834_2000_
Loop')as header(h)
 WHERE h.value('INS_MemberLevelDetail[1]/INS01_
MemberIndicator[1]'
  ,'varchar(max)') = 'Y'
)
```

Conclusion

This chapter detailed the development steps for several pipeline and pipeline components that may be useful for inbound 834 solution development. Archiving the original 834 native EDI data is essential – there will be frequent occasions when the need to reference and validate the original data will be required, and it is critical that the data is available in the exact format that the trading partners originally delivered it in. Splitting the data is also extremely valuable in many scenarios, especially when there are orchestration steps that need to take place at the subscriber level. By splitting the data at the pipeline level, and performing all metrics prior to any orchestrations, all looping and complex data handling is eliminated from orchestration development (and, in turn, this simplifies the whole process and streamlines troubleshooting and testing).

Custom Business Rules | Chapter 8

The BizTalk Rule Engine (BRE) is often looked at as an ideal option for building out business rules in BizTalk Server. However, the actual use, maintenance, and deployment of the BRE is lacking in several aspects – and when you really want to have complete control over your business rules, with the added ability to easily modify, maintain, and test these rules – the best approach is to go with a custom rules engine solution, ideally based within SQL Server. The solution outlined in Chapter 6 "Solution: Receiving 834 Data" shows the inbound 834 data being sent to a business rules stored procedure. This chapter will outline the details behind this type of implementation, and will show how to work directly with the 834 XML data to apply business rule checks. The end result of the approach outlined in this chapter is a solution that is extremely easy to test (you can do all of your work from a SQL query window) and to maintain, especially post-production (modification of a stored procedure is all that is required – no updates to DLLs, BizTalk components, schemas, etc.).

Figure 8-1 shows an overview of what the custom business rule solution looks like, and how it integrates with the inbound 834 data (this could also be applied to other document types, like the 837, if needed).

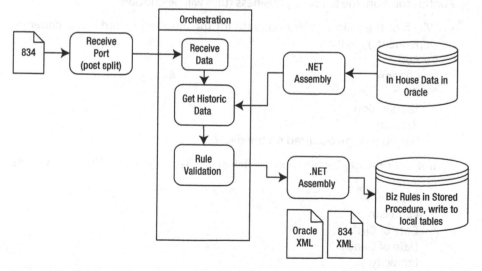

Figure 8-1. Custom Business Rule Flow

Figure 8-1 shows the basic flow for this solution. The inbound 834 arrives on the orchestration (after the split of the original 834 occurs – see Chapter 7 "Pipelines for 834 Processing" for details on splitting an 834 into individual subscriber data feeds), and there are several steps that are then taken. The first step is to do a lookup of the historical data related to this 834. The lookup in this demo will be based on the subscriber's SSN. The next step is to push both the historical XML and the current 834 XML to the business rule stored procedure for processing.

Among other things, the business rules are used to determine if the inbound data exists in the current internal database system (which means this is going to be an update to data) or if it does not exist (which means that it is an addition to the existing data). Drops, reinstates, additions, changes, terminations – whatever the 834 is saying is happening can be validated against the internal historical data. The business rules ensure that the data is handled properly – so, even if the inbound 834 says that the record is an "Update" to existing data, the business rules see that the individual never existing in the system before, so it is actually an "Add". In addition to determining what is occurring with the data, the business rules also check to see (in the case of a change) what data has changed in the current 834 from the historical data in the system.

> ■ **Note** This chapter builds on concepts outlined in Chapters 6 and 7 for the inbound 834.

The Business Rules

For this solution, the following business rules will be checked:

- Which of the following are accurate for the inbound records (subscriber or dependents) – is it an:
  - Add
  - Change
  - Drop
  - Termination
  - Reinstate
  - Has no change occurred on the data?

- If it is a Change, Termination, or Reinstate, have any of the following fields changed?
  - First Name
  - Last Name
  - Date of Birth
  - Date of Death
  - Ethnicity

The Stored Procedure

The structure of the stored procedure for this solution is as follows:

- It has two input parameters and one output parameter
  - @historicalData – this is the first input parameter, of type XML, and represents the historical data in XML format.
  - @current834 – this is the second input parameter of type XML, and it contains the 834 XML passed in from the orchestration.
  - @error – this is an output parameter of type nvarchar(max), and will contain the text of any error that occurs during the processing of the data.

- The inbound XML documents are both queried (using XQuery) for their data and the data is inserted into traditional SQL tables (in this case, temporary tables) for ease of querying and sorting.

- The inserting and updating of data (for example, the setting of flags in a table showing the outcome of the various business rule checks) is all contained within a single transaction. This ensures that the data is either fully checked, or everything is rolled back so that it can be resubmitted once the error has been addressed. If the transaction fails, and an error occurs, this error will be returned in the @error output parameter.

Listing 8-1 shows the framework for the stored procedure. The discussions in this chapter will show code that will be added to this procedure to make it a fully functional business rule processor. As code is described, the text of this chapter will say where in the following stored procedure it will need to be added. For example, the section on inserting the historical data from the XML into a temporary table will say that it should be inserted into the block [INSERT HISTORICAL HERE], which you can see in Listing 8-1 is one of the four commented sections.

Listing 8-1. Stored Procedure Framework

```
CREATE PROCEDURE [dbo].[Custom_834_Business_Rules]
(
 @historical xml
,@current xml
,@errorDescription nvarchar(max) output
)
AS
BEGIN

SET NOCOUNT ON;
DECLARE @docHandle int
      ,@currentDate datetime

SELECT @currentDate = GETDATE()
```

```
BEGIN TRAN
BEGIN TRY

-- [INSERT HISTORICAL HERE]
-- [INSERT CURRENT 834 HERE]
-- [CHECK TYPE OF RECORD]
-- [CHECK IF FIELDS HAVE CHANGED]

END TRY
BEGIN CATCH
  IF @@TRANCOUNT > 0
    ROLLBACK TRAN

  SELECT @errorNumber = ERROR_NUMBER()
        ,@errorDescription = ERROR_MESSAGE()

END CATCH
IF @@TRANCOUNT > 0
  COMMIT TRAN
```

Working with the Historical Data

For purposes of this discussion, the historical data is being queried from Oracle, transformed to XML (in this case directly from the procedure in Oracle querying the data), and is passed in as the first parameter to the stored procedure. If the historical data in your environment resides in SQL Server, then there is no need to pass it in as a separate input parameter – you can do your lookups directly against the database. If the data (such as in this case) resides in Oracle or another data model (flat file, XML, web service, etc.), then you will want to pass it in as a parameter so that you can do side by side comparisons right in the business rule stored procedure.

For purposes of illustration, the document shown in Listing 8-2 is an example of what the XML could look like from the historical data repository. Unlike the 834 XML, this XML can be tailored to any pattern of your choosing, since you have control over the structure of it. The goal is to make this structure as simplistic as possible, matching the way in which you want to work with it in the business rule comparisons. Listing 8-3 shows how to extract this information into a temporary SQL table for processing.

Only a few nodes are shown in Listings 8-2 and 8-3, as you should be able to see the pattern in how to structure and query your data. The fields that actually populate the historical temporary table (#historical) should match exactly what is populated in the field list that is pulled from the 834 (shown in Listing 8-4) so that your comparisons can be done against two identically structured tables (this isn't a requirement, but will certainly simplify your business rule logic).

Listing 8-2. Sample Historical XML Structure

```
<ResultSet>
 <MemberInfo>
  <SSN>771223333</SSN>
  <FIRSTNAME>JOHN</FIRSTNAME>
  <LASTNAME>DOE</LASTNAME>
  ...
 </MemberInfo>
 <MemberInfo>
  <SSN>001223333</SSN>
  <FIRSTNAME>JANE</FIRSTNAME>
  <LASTNAME>DOE</LASTNAME>
  ...
 </MemberInfo>
</ResultSet>
```

Listing 8-3. Extracting the Data from the Historical XML

```
-- insert this in the [INSERT HISTORICAL HERE] block of
the procedure
-- in Listing 8-1

SELECT NEWID() As ID -- give each record a temp unique ID
,T.c.query('SSN').value('.','varchar(100)') As SSN
,T.c.query('FIRSTNAME').value('.','varchar(100)') As FIRSTNAME
,T.c.query('LASTNAME').value('.','varchar(100)') As LASTNAME
INTO #Historical
FROM @historical.nodes('/ResultSet/MemberInfo') T(c)
```

Working with the Current 834 Data

The 834 XML data that is passed In as the second parameter to the stored procedure is the 834 directly from the orchestration, based on the 834 XSD. The code in Listing 8-4 shows how to pull a number of key fields from the 834 XML, and gives node paths to each (there are a variety of fields listed here to show where the data comes from in the 834 XML). The query extracts each of the unique sets of data from the inbound 834 and inserts them into a temporary table (named #current). For example, if there is one subscriber and four dependents, then there will be a total of five records inserted into the temporary table.

Listing 8-4. Extracting the Data from the 834 XML

```
-- insert this in the [INSERT CURRENT 834 HERE] block of
the procedure
-- in Listing 8-1
 SELECT NEWID() As ID -- give each record a temp unique ID

  ,T.c.query('*[local-name()=''NM1_SubLoop'']/*[local-
name()
   =''TS834_2100A_Loop'']/*[local-name()=''NM1_
MemberName'']/
   NM109_MemberIdentifier').value('.','varchar(100)') As SSN

  ,T.c.query('*[local-name()=''NM1_SubLoop'']/*[local-name()
   =''TS834_2100A_Loop'']/*[local-name()=''NM1_MemberName'']/
   NM104_MemberFirstName').value('.','varchar(100)') As
FIRSTNAME

  ,T.c.query('*[local-name()=''NM1_SubLoop'']/*[local-name()
   =''TS834_2100A_Loop'']/*[local-name()=''NM1_
MemberName'']/
   NM103_MemberLastName').value('.','varchar(100)') As
LASTNAME

  ,T.c.query('*[local-name()=''NM1_SubLoop'']/*[local-name()
   =''TS834_2100A_Loop'']/*[local-name()=''DMG_
MemberDemographics'']/
   DMG02_MemberBirthDate').value('.','varchar(100)') As
DATEOFBIRTH

  ,T.c.query('*[local-name()=''INS_
MemberLevelDetail'']/*[local-name()
   =''INS12_MemberIndividualDeathDate'']').
value('.','varchar(100)')
   As DATEOFDEATH

  ,T.c.query('*[local-name()=''NM1_SubLoop'']/*[local-name()
   =''TS834_2100A_Loop'']/*[local-name()=''DMG_
MemberDemographics'']
   /*[local-name()=''C056_
CompositeRaceorEthnicityInformation'']
   /C05601_RaceorEthnicityCode').
value('.','varchar(100)') As ETHNICITY

  ,T.c.query('*[local-name()=''TS834_2300_
Loop'']/*[local-name()
   =''DTP_HealthCoverageDates'']/*[local-name()=''DTP03_
CoveragePeriod'' and
```

```
../*[local-name()=''DTP01_DateTimeQualifier''] =
''348'']').value('.','varchar(100)') As EFFECTIVEDATE

,T.c.query('*[local-name()=''TS834_2300_
Loop'']/*[local-name()
    =''DTP_HealthCoverageDates'']/*[local-name()=''DTP03_
CoveragePeriod'' and
    ../*[local-name()=''DTP01_DateTimeQualifier''] =
    ''349'']').value('.','varchar(100)') As LIMITDATE

INTO #current
FROM @current.nodes('//*[local-name()=''TS834_2000_
Loop'']') T(c)
```

As you can see from the code in Listing 8-4, the data comes from a variety of locations in the 834 XML. Some of the nodes are obvious, others can only really be identified by referencing the 834 implementation guide specific to the trading partner(s) you are working with. Listing 8-5 shows a snippet of the 834 XML that contains the member's first name, which is one of the fields pulled in the preceding code.

Listing 8-5. A Snippet of the 834 XML Showing the Location of Member Name

```
<TS834_2000_Loop>
...
  <NM1_SubLoop>
   <TS834_2100A_Loop>
    <NM1_MemberName>
     <NM101_EntityIdentifierCode>IL</NM101_
EntityIdentifierCode>
     <NM102_EntityTypeQualifier>1</NM102_
EntityTypeQualifier>
     <NM103_MemberLastName>BOB</NM103_MemberLastName>
     <NM104_MemberFirstName>JONES</NM104_MemberFirstName>
...
```

Determining Adds, Changes, Drops, Terms, Etc.

Now that the data has been inserted into two temporary tables, it is fairly easy to do comparisons and checks for the various business rules. Some sample implementations of the rules are shown in Listings 8-6 through 8-10. As you can see, the queries are extremely simple, even though the original structure of the data was lodged in various locations in the hierarchical inbound 834 data, and comes from two different sources (historical and current). By moving this information down to the SQL level, basic data comparisons are greatly simplified over any alternative approach (including the BRE!).

> ■ **Note** The comparisons here are all based on matching on the SSN, but any field or combinations of fields that make a record unique in both the 834 XML and the historical data will work. In most cases with 834 data, you will need to come up with a combination of fields to match on, which include first name, last name, date of birth, and so on as not all records will have SSN information.

Listing 8-6. Determining Adds

```
-- insert this in the [CHECK TYPE OF RECORD] block of the
procedure
-- in Listing 8-1

-- show all records that are in the current, but not in
the historical data

SELECT A.ID As Person_ID
     ,'Add' As Type
FROM #historical A
WHERE A.SSN NOT IN (SELECT B.SSN FROM #current B)
```

Listing 8-7. Determining Drops

```
-- insert this in the [CHECK TYPE OF RECORD] block of the
procedure
-- in Listing 8-1

-- show all records that are in the historical, but not
in the current data

SELECT A.ID As Person_ID
     ,'Drop' As Type
FROM #historical A
WHERE A.SSN NOT IN (SELECT B.SSN FROM #current B)
AND DATEDIFF(DAY, @currentDate, A.LIMITDATE) >= 0
-- only want those with limit dates in the future
```

Listing 8-8. Determining Terminations

```
-- insert this in the [CHECK TYPE OF RECORD] block of the
procedure
-- in Listing 8-1
```

```
SELECT A.ID As Person_ID
       ,'Termination' As Type
FROM #current A
LEFT JOIN #historical B ON A.SSN = B.SSN
WHERE DATEDIFF(DAY, @currentDate, B.LIMITDATE) >= 0
-- only want those with limit dates in the future
AND DATEDIFF(DAY, A.LIMITDATE, B.LIMITDATE) != 0
-- limits must be different
```

Listing 8-9. Checking if the First Name has Changed

```
-- insert this in the [CHECK IF FIELDS HAVE CHANGED]
block of the procedure
-- in Listing 8-1

SELECT A.ID As Person_ID
       ,'First Name Changed' As Flag
FROM #current A
LEFT JOIN #historical B ON A.SSN = B.SSN
WHERE CASE WHEN A.FIRSTNAME = B.FIRSTNAME THEN 0 ELSE 1
END = 1
```

Listing 8-10. Checking if the Ethnicity has Changed

```
-- insert this in the [CHECK IF FIELDS HAVE CHANGED]
block of the procedure
-- in Listing 8-1

SELECT A.ID As Person_ID
       ,'Ethnicity Changed' As Flag
FROM #current A
LEFT JOIN #historical B ON A.SSN = B.SSN
WHERE CASE WHEN A.ETHNICITY = B.ETHNICITY THEN 0 ELSE 1
END = 1
```

Testing the Stored Procedure

Because the two input parameters to the stored procedure are XML, it can be a little tricky to test the stored procedure. Listing 8-11 shows one approach, which can be executed directly from a SQL query window. This is a great way to test, as you can alter the XML easily and test the results of the stored procedure without having to write any external code. However, you may decide you want a more robust test harness – in which case writing a simple C# forms application will be the next best approach. Try to stay out of BizTalk while testing this portion of the code, as it will only add overhead to your processing and validation activities.

Listing 8-11. Testing the Stored Procedure

```
DECLARE @historical xml
       ,@current xml
       ,@errorDescription varchar(max)
SELECT @historical = '<pasteHistoricalXMLHere/>'

SELECT @current = '<pasteCurrentXMLHere/>'

EXEC Custom_834_Business_Rules @historical, @current,
@errorDescription out

SELECT @errorDescription
```

Handling Business Rule Execution Results

The business rules are simple to work through – but you must determine what you want to do with the results. For example, if you have an inbound 834 that has one subscriber who has no change to the data, and three dependents (one add, one change, and one reinstate), how do you handle these records?

One approach is to write to a series of tables in SQL at the end of the stored procedure, and let further processing occur to move this data into the target environment. Another approach is to return an XML document to the original calling orchestration so that it can continue to process things as needed. Figure 8-2 illustrates the flow to several potential options around the continued processing of this data.

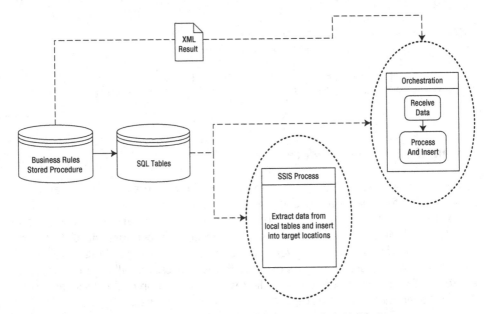

Figure 8-2. Potential Options for Processing After Business Rule Validations

The goal is to ensure that you are doing things with the least amount of code, and in the most efficient way possible. Obviously, you will need to have a strategy before you ever begin your business rules architecture. Much will depend on how your internal data is structured, and how your business needs to deal with the various entities.

Calling the Stored Procedure from the Orchestration

Calling the stored procedure is done using a C# method in a .NET helper class, referenced by the orchestration. There is no need to use any type of adapter, as adapters just add complexity and overhead to most solutions. Listing 8-12 shows the basic code for calling the stored procedure, passing in two parameters of type XML, and getting back an error message.

Listing 8-12. C# Method Called from Orchestration to Execute Stored Procedure

```
public void callBusinessRules(string historicalXML,
string currentXML, out
 string strErrorDescription)
{
 currentXML = currentXML.Replace("encoding=\"utf-8\"", "");
 string connection =
  System.Configuration.ConfigurationManager.AppSettings
["ConnectionStringKey"];
 string sproc = "Custom_834_Business_Rules";

 SqlConnection sqlConnection = new
SqlConnection(connection);
 sqlConnection.Open();
 SqlCommand sqlCommand = new SqlCommand(sproc,
sqlConnection);
 sqlCommand.CommandType = CommandType.StoredProcedure;

 SqlParameter parameterHistXML = new SqlParameter();
 parameterHistXML.Direction = ParameterDirection.Input;
 parameterHistXML.ParameterName = "@historical";
 parameterHistXML.SqlDbType = SqlDbType.Xml;
 parameterHistXML.Value = historicalXML;
 sqlCommand.Parameters.Add(parameterHistXML);

 SqlParameter parameterCurrXML = new SqlParameter();
 parameterCurrXML.Direction = ParameterDirection.Input;
 parameterCurrXML.ParameterName = "@current";
 parameterCurrXML.SqlDbType = SqlDbType.Xml;
 parameterCurrXML.Value = currentXML;
 sqlCommand.Parameters.Add(parameterCurrXML);
```

```
SqlParameter parameterErrorDesc = new SqlParameter();
parameterErrorDesc.Direction = ParameterDirection.
Output;
parameterErrorDesc.DbType = DbType.String;
parameterErrorDesc.Size = -1;
parameterErrorDesc.ParameterName = "@errorDescription";
sqlCommand.Parameters.Add(parameterErrorDesc);

SqlDataReader reader = sqlCommand.ExecuteReader();

strErrorDescription =
  sqlCommand.Parameters["@errorDescription"].Value.
ToString();

sqlConnection.Close();
}
```

Conclusion

The purpose of this chapter was to walk through an example of implementing an easy to maintain, highly customizable approach to business rule management that is common to inbound 834 implementations. By using a SQL Server stored procedure, and housing all of the rules in SQL, the rules engine becomes a tool that can be developed and modified by virtually any resource – most developers know T-SQL. It also is something that can be tested and changed on the fly, with no reliance on compiled or deployed code. If a rule needs to change after the solution has been deployed to production, it is as easy as modifying a procedure. Looking at a highly maintainable, easy to use business rule engine will be a relief, compared with

Advanced 834 Mapping ⬛ Chapter 9

Depending on what trading partner you are integrating with, and what the requirements are of your integration, you may find that there are some complexities to the architecture required to deliver a fully functional solution. One such pattern that is very common, yet can be difficult to build out, is related to the outbound 834 maintenance (or effectuation/reconciliation). The pattern here is that the outbound 834 data must contain all of the original inbound 834 information related to a specific subscriber/dependent along with all of the updated information from an internal system. The complexity here lies in the fact that in general, the inbound 834 data is not mapped in its entirety to a backend system within an organization. There are aspects to the data that are irrelevant to internal processes, and often have no place to be stored. In this case, the original 834 data must be stored so that it can be referenced at a later time when the outbound data ships out.

Figure 9-1 gives a high-level overview of what this architecture looks like, and this chapter will describe the components used, the most critical of which is the outbound 834 map. This map is probably unlike any map you've done in the past. It allows for multiple lookups and handles looping – items that are traditionally relegated to orchestrations or other components. By handling it in the map, the outbound flow of data can rely on a simple base of components, and will allow for grouping and batching of data based on trading partner requirements.

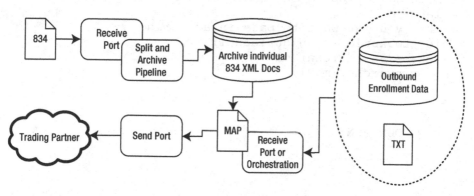

Figure 9-1. High-Level Overview of Data Flow

Inbound Components

Chapters 6, 7, and 8 have gone into detail about various components for inbound processing. The only thing that deserves mention about the architecture here is the writing of the 837 XML to a database table. The purpose of writing the individually split XML documents to a table is to ensure that this original data can be referenced and pulled from the outbound map. In this case, you will need to add a unique identifier to the row where the XML is written, so that it can be easily cross referenced from the outbound data. For example, if SSN is a unique identifier which will be available on all records, you could use that. More than likely, it will need to be a combination of the group policy number and the member number, which you will need to pull out of the XML data itself in order to capture it in its own fields in the table. There may be some cases where you will have no unique field within the data, and you'll have to create a unique identifier (GUID) and store it not only in this lookup/archive table, but also in your target data repository, so that it can be sent out and used to repopulate the data on the outbound portion of the process.

The table for the inbound data which houses the 834 XML should look similar to that shown in Figure 9-2. An example of writing this data to a table using C# and a stored procedure is shown in Listings 9-1 and 9-2.

	ID	UniqueLookupID	834_XML	OriginalFileName	CreateDate
1	E17D963E-918...	567898761	cns0:X12_00501_834 xmlns.ns0="http://schemas.mic...	C:\Inbound\83411292013100607.txt	2013-11-26

Figure 9-2. Inbound 834 XML Lookup Table Structure

Listing 9-1. Stored Procedure to Archive 834 XML for Lookup

```
CREATE PROCEDURE ArchiveEDI
-- you can pass your XML as a varchar or as xml.
-- If you want to do pre-processing on the string
-- such as stripping out characters or doing string
replaces,
-- then you may want to pass in as string
@UniqueLookupId as uniqueidentifier,
@FileName as nvarchar(max),
@XML as nvarchar(max),

AS
BEGIN
 SET NOCOUNT ON;
```

```
-- do REPLACE operations here, perhaps on namespaces,
ns0:, etc.
  INSERT INTO [X834_Archived]
  (ID
  ,UniqueLookupID
  ,834_XML
  ,OriginalFileName
  ,CreateDate
  )
  VALUES
  (NEWID()
  ,@UniqueLookupID
  ,CAST(@XML as xml)
  ,@FileName
  ,GETDATE()
  )
END
```

Listing 9-2. C# Called from Orchestration/Pipeline to Call Stored Procedure

```csharp
public void ArchiveEdi(string fileName, string xml,
string uniqueLookupID)
{
  string strConnection =
   System.Configuration.ConfigurationManager.
AppSettings["EDI.Database"];
  string sproc = "ArchiveEDI";

  SqlConnection sqlConnection = new
SqlConnection(strConnection);
  sqlConnection.Open();
  SqlCommand sqlCommand = new SqlCommand(sproc,
sqlConnection);
  sqlCommand.CommandType = CommandType.StoredProcedure;

  SqlParameter parameterID = new SqlParameter();
  parameterID.Direction = ParameterDirection.Input;
  parameterID.ParameterName = "@UniqueLookupId";
  parameterID.Value = new Guid(uniqueLookupID);
  sqlCommand.Parameters.Add(parameterUniqueLookupID);

  SqlParameter parameterFileName = new SqlParameter();
  parameterFileName.Direction = ParameterDirection.Input;
  parameterFileName.ParameterName = "@FileName";
  parameterFileName.Value = fileName;
  sqlCommand.Parameters.Add(parameterFileName);
```

```
SqlParameter parameterXML = new SqlParameter();
parameterXML.Direction = ParameterDirection.Input;
parameterXML.ParameterName = "@XML";
parameterXML.Value = xml;
sqlCommand.Parameters.Add(parameterXML);

sqlCommand.ExecuteNonQuery();
sqlConnection.Close();
}
```

Outbound Components

The outbound components for this solution include the stored procedure or text file that consists of the data making up the source enrollment information (which represents the internal data stored within your company's systems), the map which maps the internal data to the target 834 schema and also does the lookup of data from the original 834 inbound archived data, and the standard BizTalk artifacts (party configurations, receive and send ports, etc.).

Source Data

The source data can come in a variety of forms, including database result set, flat file, and XML file. Your ideal scenario is to get the data into an XML format prior to delivering to BizTalk. Pulling an XML formatted result set from the database has been discussed in Chapter 3 "Solution: Sending 837P Data", and is a critical component for simple architectures. For example, if you can retrieve data in XML, you can often eliminate orchestrations from your solution entirely. In the case of the current solution, we are pulling data from two sources – the data that is coming in and represents the outbound enrollment data and also the original inbound 834 that contains the remainder of the required 834 information. Though there are two documents and multiple database calls, there is no need for an orchestration. Given the complexity of the mapping, eliminating other components allows you (the developer) to focus your energies entirely on mapping and not on building unnecessary components.

> **Note** One common approach to pulling data in XML from a database and rendering it in a file format for ease of pickup from BizTalk is to create an SSIS process. This process formats the data and writes it to a file on a directory where BizTalk is listening using a standard File Receive location.

Listing 9-3 shows an example of outbound enrollment data that represents the source data which can come from either a file drop or an XML query from a database. This data contains all of the information that the internal system stored related to enrollment information, but it does not contain all of the information required in the mapping of the outbound 834 data. The remainder of this data will come from the original archived 834 data which was written as shown above in Figure 9-1, and would be looked up using the UniqueLookupID in the XML (this could also be a combination of standard fields like SSN, member ID, name, etc.).

Listing 9-3. Sample Outbound Enrollment Data

```
<Enrollments>
 <Enrollment>
  <TargetTradingPartnerID>{name of destination party in
BizTalk parties}
  </TargetTradingPartnerID>
  <Subscriber>
   <UniqueLookupID>{this matches what is in Figure 9-1}
</UniqueLookupID>
   <MemberID>1112223333</MemberID>
   <FirstName>John</FirstName>
   <LastName>Doe</LastName>
   <Dependents>
    <Dependent>
     <FirstName>Jane</FirstName>
     <LastName>Doe</LastName>
 . . .
```

The Map

The map, which consists of the source data schema and the target 834 XSD, will consist of two functoids. The first functoid is a global C# Inline Scripting functoid and the second is an XSLT Inline Scripting functoid (see Chapter 4 "Mapping Data" for details around both of these concepts). The XSLT creates the target schema line by line, and uses C# to retrieve the data, format the data, and determine whether the target data values come from the source data or from the original 834 lookup data. Figure 9-3 shows the map.

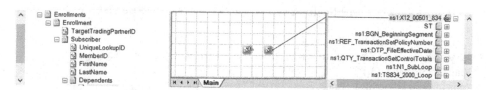

Figure 9-3. The Map with All Functoids

The XSLT Scripting functoid is where most of the code for this mapping solution is at. For nodes that must be mapped in the target 834, and for which data exists in the source data schema (Enrollments, on the left side of the map in Figure 9-3), data can be mapped using standard XSLT. For nodes that are not in the source data, but must be looked up in the original 834 archived XML, data can be mapped using the $original834Enrollment parameter and the GetNode inline C# method. Listing 9-4 shows sample XSLT for mapping some of the member information in the 834 using data from both the source schema and the original 834 lookup data. Listing 9-5 shows the GetNode method, which allows for a source document along with the specific XPath to the node to be passed in and returns the string value (if the node is found).

Listing 9-4. Populating the Member Information in the 834

```
<xsl:element name ="TS834_2100A_Loop">
 <xsl:element name ="NM1_MemberName">
  <NM101_EntityIdentifierCode>
   <xsl:value-of select="userCSharp:GetNode(
    $original834Enrollment,'//*/*/*/*[local-
    name()=&quot;NM101_EntityIdentifierCode&quot;]')"/>
  </NM101_EntityIdentifierCode>
  <NM102_EntityTypeQualifier>
   <xsl:value-of select="userCSharp:GetNode(
    $original834Enrollment,'//*/*/*/*[local-
    name()=&quot;NM102_EntityTypeQualifier&quot;]')"/>
  </NM102_EntityTypeQualifier>
  <NM103_MemberLastName>
   <xsl:value-of select ="./*/*[local-
name()='LastName']"/>
  </NM103_MemberLastName>
  <xsl:if test ="./*/*[local-name()='FirstName']">
   <NM104_MemberFirstName>
    <xsl:value-of select ="./*/*[local-
name()='FirstName']"/>
   </NM104_MemberFirstName>
  </xsl:if>
```

Listing 9-5. The GetNode Inline C# Function

```
public string GetNode(string xml ,string xpath)
{
 string result ="";
 System.Xml.XmlDocument xmlDoc = new System.Xml.
XmlDocument();
 xmlDoc.LoadXml(xml.Replace("ns0:", ""));
 System.Xml.XmlNode node;
```

```
System.Xml.XmlElement root = xmlDoc.DocumentElement;
node = root.SelectSingleNode(path);

if (node!=null)
{
 result = node.InnerXml;
}

return result;
}
```

Listing 9-4 uses the $original834Enrollment parameter, which is populated in the Inline XSLT through the code shown in Listing 9-6. It uses a C# method in the BizTalk helper assembly (rather than in the Inline C#) to do this, as it is a database lookup that is performed. Referencing a .NET assembly method from Inline XSLT requires two additional steps – the first is the creation of an XML document (referenced in your Visual Studio file) that is an Extension Object which tells the XSLT where to find the assembly (an example of this is shown in Listing 9-7). This XML file must then be referenced in the map properties in the Custom Extension XML property, as shown in Figure 9-4.

Listing 9-6. Retrieving the Original 834 XML in XSLT

```
<xsl:variable name="original834Enrollment"
xmlns:CompanyNS="http://companyname.com/xslt/
extensions" select="CompanyNS:getEdiMessage($lookup,'Data
Source=MDB;Initial Catalog=CompanyLookup;User Id=BTServic
e;Password=123pass')" />
```

> ■ **Note** The PublicKeyToken in Listing 9-7 should match the key on your assembly. You can get this value from the properties in the GAC.

Listing 9-7. Custom Extension XML

```
(for Referencing External Assembly)
<ExtensionObjects>
 <ExtensionObject Namespace="http://companyname.com/xslt/
extensions"
  AssemblyName="Company.BizTalk.Utilities,
Version=1.0.0.0, Culture=neutral,
  PublicKeyToken=eeee12345678b123" ClassName="Company.
BizTalk.Utilities.Helper"
 />
</ExtensionObjects>
```

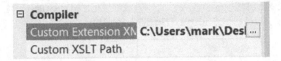

Figure 9-4. Referencing the Custom Extension XML

> ■ **Note**   Click on any white space on the map surface in order to access the properties where the Customer Extension XML property can be set.

The C# code used in the external assembly to do the original lookup of the 834 XML is shown in Listing 9-8.

Listing 9-8. External Assembly XML Lookup

```
public static string GetEDIMessage(string uniqueLookupID)
{
 string result = string.Empty;
 string sproc = "GetOriginal834";
 string connectionString = //pull this from the config
file or other location

 using (SqlConnection connection = new SqlConnection(conn
ectionString))
  {
   using (SqlCommand cmd = connection.CreateCommand())
   {
    cmd.CommandText = sproc;
    cmd.CommandType = CommandType.StoredProcedure;
    connection.Open();

    SqlParameter paramReferenceNumber = new
SqlParameter();
    paramReferenceNumber.ParameterName =
"@UniqueLookupID";
    paramReferenceNumber.Direction = ParameterDirection
.Input;
    paramReferenceNumber.Value = uniqueLookupID;
    cmd.Parameters.Add(paramReferenceNumber);
    var scalar = cmd.ExecuteScalar();
    result = scalar as string;
   }
  }
 return result;
}
```

Ports/Party Configuration/Etc.

It is possible to create an outbound 834 solution that does not use an orchestration, and relies solely on ports, pipelines, and maps. The solution outlined in this chapter can take this approach, as long as the source data is delivered in a file drop (or similar) format in XML. In this case, it is a receive port/location that picks up the XML, along with a map that transforms the source XML into an EDI 834 document. Configuring the trading partner's agreement and party settings in BizTalk, along with send ports and filters, will determine how the data is routed and processed. There are a number of examples of routing outbound data, shown in Chapters 10 and 11.

Conclusion

A complex architectural requirement – using archived historical data and source data to create a target 834 without the use of an orchestration – has been outlined in this solution. The advanced mapping required to handle this scenario takes some forethought, and relies heavily on XSLT, and requires integration with C# Inline scripts and an external C# assembly, but allows for substantial freedom in development. Being able to use these advanced mapping techniques will come in handy as you work through receiving and sending your 834 data. The next two chapters will focus on patterns for sending this data, and you can determine how best to incorporate your mapping into these solutions.

You have looked at sending and receiving 837 data (in Chapters 2 and 3) and also at receiving 834 data (Chapter 6). There are several additional concepts to introduce, most notably the use of role links. The solution in this chapter will show how to receive flat file data on a receive port, map that data to an outbound 834 document, and use role links to send to a specific trading partner. You will look at options for how to use an adapter to pull data from an SFTP server, how to structure the source data you'll be mapping from, and how to configure role links to allow for sending to any number of trading partners dynamically from within an orchestration. The architectural overview of this solution is shown in Figure 10-1.

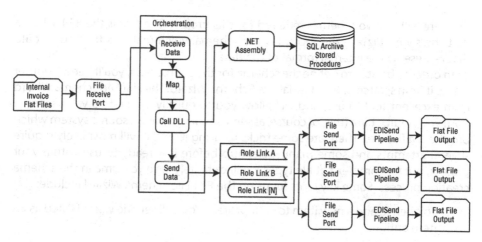

Figure 10-1. Outbound 834 Solution Overview

Visual Studio Solution

As discussed in the previous solution-based chapters, namespaces and project structure are essential to a successful project, so always take time in the beginning to think through all of the components that will be required and how best to name and organize them. Trying to change namespaces and project organization later in the development cycle is especially frustrating with BizTalk, given the number of components and complexity of testing. For this solution, the following Visual Studio projects and namespaces will be used:

- Solution Name: Company.BizTalk. You can use the same solution you used for the project in Chapter 6 "Solution: Receiving 834 Data."

- Schemas. There are two schemas that will be used in this solution, as follows. The name of this project is Company.BizTalk.Schemas.X834. You can reuse the project from Chapter 6 here, and just include the additional schema.
  - ° The 834 Schema. This is the target schema that will be mapped to and sent out.
  - ° The Source Schema. This schema represents the internal representation of the enrollment data.

- Maps. The map project will contain a single map with logic to create an 834 from the source data, and will have a namespace of Company.BizTalk. Maps.X834.

The Schema Project

There will be two schemas required for this project. The first is the 834 schema that ships with BizTalk, the second is the schema which matches the source data that represents the internal format of the data.

In order to be able to define the schema for the source data, you'll need to either create it from scratch or use the Flat File Schema Wizard. The Flat File Schema Wizard is an excellent tool to use, and will allow you to quickly generate a valid schema from your source data (this, of course, assumes that you have a source system which produces a flat file). There are some tricks to using it, and it will most likely require several attempts and some manual cleanup before it is ready to use within your project, but for complex flat file types it will definitely save you time in the schema creation process. Some key hints for using the Flat File Schema Wizard include:

- To open it, add a new item to your project. You will see the wizard listed as an item option.

- You will need a valid flat file instance to point to in order for the wizard to generate an instance. Make sure and choose a sample instance that has enough data in it to ensure that all possible formatting combinations are represented (such as columns with null values, the presence of parent and child records, etc.).

- The final output of the Wizard is often two or more schemas; one will reference the other. Ideally, you will have a single schema that represents your source data, so if you have the patience to manually convert this into a single schema, you will save yourself time and frustration during the mapping process.

- If you already have a flat file schema that is similar to the format of your new source data, you should probably start by copying this and modifying it, rather than using the wizard. For example, if you have a schema that represents flat file data in a comma delineated format with line returns separating each record, and your new source schema has pipes for the separator and a number of additional columns, then it will be quicker to modify a copy of the existing schema than to work through the wizard.

The Map Project

You will have a single map for the outbound process, which will map the source data to the target 834 structure. Details for mapping are given in Chapter 4 "Mapping Data", while advanced concepts for mapping the 834 are shown in Chapter 9 "Advanced 834 Mapping".

The map project structure should be as follows:

- Create/reuse a new project in Visual Studio called Company.BizTalk. Maps.X834.

- Add a reference to the schema project you just created earlier in this chapter.

The .NET Helper Library Project

You will need a C# assembly for any of the database interactions that are done from the map or from the orchestration. Generally speaking, steer clear of using the SQL adapters for communication with the database, unless you have a very specific requirement such as polling on a timed basis. The adapters add a lot of unnecessary weight to a solution, and communicating through the use of C# and an assembly keeps things simple and easy to modify and maintain. A good discussion about the .NET library helper class can be found in Chapter 2 "Solution: Receiving 837P Data." For the purposes of this demo, the library is used for lookups in the map and for archiving data to the database (which is outlined in full in Chapter 2). It is also used to determine the name of the party so that the orchestration can use role links to send the data.

The Orchestration Project

The process that will be taken for outbound 834s in the orchestration is shown in the following bulleted list (Figure 10-2 shows the orchestration in full). The details behind each of the shapes is also given in this section.

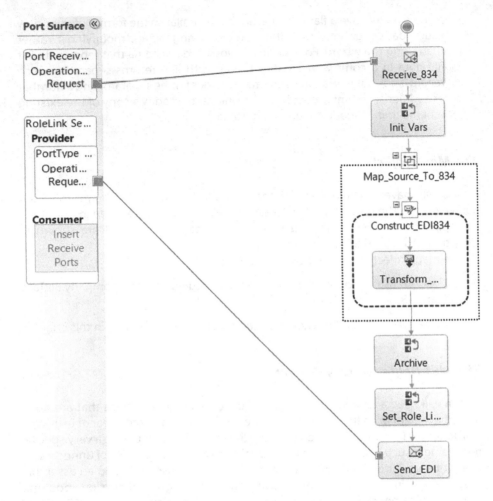

Figure 10-2. The Orchestration

- The internal representation of enrollment data is posted via a file drop, and the orchestration picks this up. The enrollment could be for any trading partner, the identification of the trading partner that will receive the document is contained in the data itself. This data will be used at the end of the orchestration to correlate the outbound message with a specific role link and party.

- The data will be mapped to the 834 EDI format, archived, and sent to the appropriate destination using the role link.

The Receive_834 Shape

This is the initial shape that instantiates the orchestration. When a flat file arrives on the port, the orchestration will be activated (set the Activate property on this shape to True). Create a message called msgSource and set the type of it to the source flat file schema defined in your schema project.

The Init_Vars Shape

The code in this shape has a number of lookups, and sets several variables to values from the inbound file that have been promoted for use. The lookups are for fields that are used in setting the appropriate outbound party for the role link and for overriding the GS02, if necessary. The code, with notes, is shown in Listing 10-1.

Listing 10-1. Init_Vars Expression Shape Code

```
// these fields are set here so that they can be easily
written to the database
strType = "834 Outbound";
strTradingPartnerID = msgSource.RecordEnvelope.Line.
CustomerID;
strReceivedFileName = msgSource(FILE.ReceivedFileName);
strLocationCode = msgSource.RecordEnvelope.Line.
AddressCode;

// now get the public location code - this is a simple
database lookup that
// uses a method in the helper library.
strLocationCode =
objHelper.LookupCustomerLocationCode(strTradingPartnerID,
strLocationCode);

// get the party name so that the role link can be set.
This is another
// simple lookup that uses a method in the helper
assembly.
strPartyName =
objHelper.LookupCustomerInfo("vchPartyName","ST",
strLocationCode);

// get the GS02, in case it needs to be overridden.
Another lookup.
strGS02 =
objHelper.LookupCustomerInfo("vchGS02","ST",strLocationCode);
```

Make sure and review the additional notes around how the Init_Vars shape can be used to read from a configuration file as outlined in Chapter 2.

The Map_Source_to_834 Shape

This references the map that was created in the mapping project earlier in this chapter. The input is msgSource and the output can go into a message called msgEDI834 (and should be the 834 schema type).

The Archive Shape

This is basically the same process for archiving as was outlined in Chapter 2. The code within this shape simply takes an XML document and some additional parameters (like the document type, the party name, etc.) and passes it to a method in the helper assembly, which in turn writes the information to a SQL table.

The Set_RoleLink Shape

Since every outbound enrollment data structure is delivered to this orchestration, the orchestration has to determine who the receiving party is going to be. For example, say that there are ten trading partners who receive enrollment data, all on different FTP sites with different envelope information. If role links were not used, the orchestration logic would require ten different ports just to send the data, let alone determine the envelope settings and party to associate it with. Using role links allows the orchestration to have a single outbound port, and uses the settings in the configured role links and party settings to distribute the data to the correct target party.

The code for this shape is shown here:

```
RoleLink_Send834(Microsoft.XLANGs.BaseTypes.
DestinationParty) =
new Microsoft.XLANGs.BaseTypes.Party(strPartyName,
"OrganizationName");
```

This sets the value of the destination party (which will match the name of the role link to use, configured later in the BizTalk Admin console) that will be used to send the data. In order for this to work, you will need to take the following steps to configure the role link. The role link will act and look very similar to a send port.

1. On the port surface of your orchestration, right click and select New Role Link. In the wizard that pops up, do the following:

   a. Set the name – for this Demo, it can be set to RoleLink_Send834.

   b. Create a new Role Link Type. The name can be PortType_Send_EDI834

   c. Set the role link to "Provider."

   d. Create a port type within the Provider role link that is set to the Send_EDI834 port type, has one-way communication and public access.

2. Create a new Role Link Type in the orchestration view of your orchestration, and link it to the role link "port" you created in the previous step.

The Send_EDI Shape

This shape needs to be set to the outbound message created from the map (the 834 EDI) and connected to the Provider type on the role link. The type of message should match the outbound port type within the Provider role link.

The Pipeline Project

The final project required is a simple custom flat file pipeline using the Flat File Disassembler component that ships with BizTalk. The use of this pipeline on a Receive Port will allow the inbound source document to be converted from the flat file format into XML. Figure 10-3 shows this pipeline. The steps to create this pipeline are as follows:

- Create a new project called Company.BizTalk.Outbound.Pipelines.X834.

- Add a new Receive Pipeline to this project.

- In the pipeline GUI interface, drop a Flat File Disassembler component on the Disassemble stage.

- In the properties of the disassembler component, set the Document Schema property to the Company.BizTalk.Schemas.X834 schema created earlier in this project (you may have to deploy the schema DLL in order to have access to this).

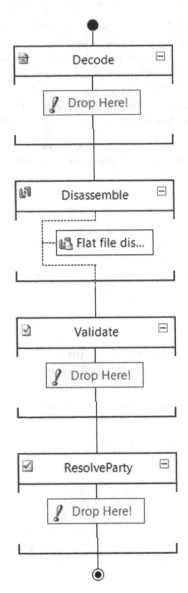

Figure 10-3. The Flat File Pipeline and Disassembler Component

Setting up the BizTalk Components

For this solution, you will need to set up the receive port and receive location, bind the orchestration, and configure the role link settings.

Before configuring these components, you will want to deploy your Visual Studio assemblies to the BizTalk Application. Steps for doing this are outlined in Chapter 2.

File Receive Port

The input to this solution is a simple File Receive Port. A flat file will arrive on a file drop and will be picked up by the orchestration. This receive location associated with this port needs to have the pipeline created earlier in this chapter associated with it, so that it can process the flat file.

- Create a new Receive Port and Receive Location combination, both named Company.BizTalk.Receive.Enrollment.FlatFile.

- Set the Type to File and point it to the directory where the flat files will be dropped.

- Set the Receive Pipeline to Company.BizTalk.Outbound.Pipelines.X834.

SFTP Send Ports

Each trading partner can receive their data via any protocol they require. In this case, you will look at configuring an SFTP Send Port. This port will be associated with the BizTalk party, and will be triggered from the orchestration through the role link that you will soon configure. There will be one send port created for each trading partner. In order to illustrate role links, two trading partners will be set up, so two send ports will need to be configured for this demo.

- Create two new Send Ports named Company.BizTalk.Send.TradingPartner_A and Company.BizTalk.Send.TradingPartner_B.

- Set the Type to SFTP. Details for configuring the SFTP adapter are given in Chapter 5.

- Set the Send Pipeline to EdiSend.

■ **Note**   A single send port can be used to send numerous EDI transaction types. You are configuring these for the 834, but if you were to deliver more transaction types (such as an 837, for example) you would not need to configure a new port – unless the actual physical location that is being delivered to is different for the various document types.

Party Settings

In the previous chapter, you looked at configuring the base settings for the BizTalk Party and Agreement on inbound data. You can reuse these settings, or you can configure fresh trading partners. The home organization can remain the same. The basics of what you will want are as follows (Figure 10-4 shows a high-level summary of parties and agreements).

- Three trading partners. One representing the home organization (your company), and one for each of the recipient organizations that the 834 EDI documents are being sent to.

- Two agreements, one for each recipient organization.

- In the agreements, the critical information to configure is as follows

  ° The Identifiers tab must be set up on both the inbound and outbound settings.

  ° The Send Port tab on the outbound settings (Home Company ➤ Trading Partner) must have a reference to the SFTP Send Port configured earlier in this chapter. Make sure that the send port you are setting up corresponds to the party you are configuring the agreement for.

  ° The Envelope tab must have the information for the 834 transaction type configured.

    - Transaction Type should be 834-Benefit Enrollment and Maintenance

    - Version is set to 00401 (match your correct version).

    - Target namespace should be `http://schemas.microsoft.com/BizTalk/EDI/X12/2006`

    - GS1 should be BE-Benefit Enrollment and Maintenance (834)

    - GS2 through GS7 should be set based on what your trading partner requires (see the trading partner implementation guide or a sample 834 instance from them)

    - GS8 should be 004010 (or 005010 for 5010, you will need to match the right version).

Note The role links work in conjunction with the parties, and whatever send port is associated with the party in the agreements (and corresponds to the type of data being sent) will be used to send the physical file.

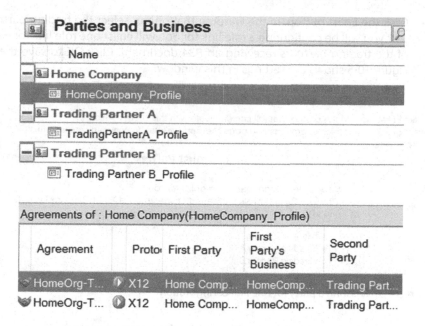

Figure 10-4. Parties and Agreements

Configuring the Role Links

The final step for this solution is the set up and configuration of the role links. The orchestration is set to pick up enrollment data that could be delivered to any trading partner in the 834 format. For the purposes of this demo, two trading partners have been configured, but in real-world scenarios you may be required to set up dozens of trading partners, all receiving the 834 transaction type. For each trading partner, you will need to:

- Configure a BizTalk party and create a new agreement (this is where the envelope and other information unique to a trading partner is configured).

- Set up a send port. A send port can be used to send multiple EDI document types (834, 837, etc.), but each trading partner will need to have its own dedicated send port.

- Set up a role link. This enables the orchestration to dynamically send to the appropriate target party.

To set up a role link, take these steps:

- Open the BizTalk Admin console and click on Role Links in the Company. BizTalk application.

- In the right-hand pane, double click the Provider option (this represents parties that will be sent to).

- Click the Enlist button. In the window that opens, select the trading partner that you will be configuring a role link for. You will enlist one role link for each of the trading partners receiving an 834 document. Click OK to save these. Figure 10-5 shows the settings in this window.

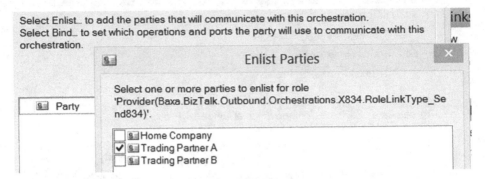

Figure 10-5. Enlisting a party for role link configuration

- Back in the main window, double click each party to bind them.

- In the window that opens for binding, select the send port to associate with the orchestration's port operation. This send port should be unique to the trading partner (although it can be used for multiple document types). Figure 10-6 shows this binding for a trading partner.

Bind Party to Role

When binding a party to a role, you must specify ports for communication.

Role: Provider(BizTalk.Outbound.Orchestrations.X834.RoleLinkTy

Party: Trading Partner A

Bindings:

Operation	Send Port
Port Type:	BizTalk.Outbound.Orchestrations.X834.PortType_Send
Operation_1 (One way)	Trading Partner A - 834

Figure 10-6. Binding the party to a role

- Once you have the role links fully configured, the orchestration will be able to utilize them.

- The orchestration binds to the role link using the party name. For example, if the role link shows "Trading Partner A" as the party name when it is has been bound, the orchestration must refer to it with this name. So – in the Set_RoleLink shape of the orchestration you created earlier in this chapter, the code would be:

  ° RoleLink_Send834(Microsoft.XLANGs.BaseTypes.DestinationParty) =

  ° new Microsoft.XLANGs.BaseTypes.Party("Trading Partner A", "OrganizationName");

Enabling and Running the Solution

In order for this solution to work, the Receive Location must be enabled, the Send Ports must be started, and the orchestration must be running. You will want to restart the BizTalk Host Instance to ensure that all of the most recent configurations and components are loaded into memory.

Conclusion

This chapter covered some critical aspects of developing BizTalk EDI solutions using some advanced BizTalk concepts. You will likely find that the requirements for your specific implementation vary from the specific pattern outlined in this solution, but you should have more than enough information now to be able to architect an efficient and highly maintainable outbound solution. The next chapter will discuss the same outbound 834 flow, with all of the advanced components stripped out. This will allow you to compare the various styles of development and the required components for various architectures.

Solution: Sending 834 - Simplified

The previous chapter outlined an outbound 834 solution that had a number of components (orchestration, role links, etc.) and steps. You will now look at a solution that uses only schemas, ports, maps, and party configurations. The architectural overview of this solution is shown in Figure 11-1.

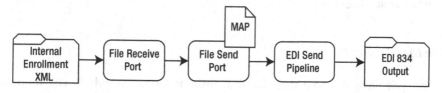

Figure 11-1. Outbound 834 Simplified Solution Overview.

> ■ **Note** This chapter builds on concepts outlined in the previous solution-based chapters, and assumes knowledge of foundational concepts and best practices that have already been outlined.

Visual Studio Solution

For this solution, the following Visual Studio projects and namespaces will be used:

- Solution Name: Company.BizTalk. You can use the same solution you used for the 834 projects in the earlier chapters, or you can create a new one.

- Schemas. There are two schemas that will be used in this solution, as follows. The name of this project is Company.BizTalk.Schemas.X834.

- ° The 834 Schema. This is the target schema that will be mapped to and sent out.
- ° The Source Schema. This schema represents the internal representation of the enrollment data.
- Maps. The map project will contain a single map with logic to create an 834 from the source data, and will have a namespace of Company.BizTalk. Maps.X834.

The Schema Project

There will be two schemas required for this project. The first is the 834 schema that ships with BizTalk, the second is the schema representing the internal format of the enrollment data. For this solution, it will be an XML document dropped on a file drop. In a real-world scenario, this XML could be generated by an SSIS process, or other similar process.

The Map Project

You will have a single map for the outbound process, which will map the source data to the target 834 structure. Details for mapping are given in Chapter 4 "Mapping Data," while advanced concepts for 834 mapping are outlined in Chapter 9 "Advanced 834 Mapping."

The map project structure should be as follows:

- Create a new project in Visual Studio called Demo.BizTalk.Maps.X834.
- Add a reference to the schema project you have created.

Setting up the BizTalk Components

For this solution, you will need to set up the receive port and receive location, and configure a send port to subscribe to this receive port.

Before configuring these components, you will want to deploy your Visual Studio assemblies to the BizTalk Application. Steps for doing this are outlined in Chapter 2 "Solution: Receiving 837P Data."

File Receive Port

The input to this solution is a simple File Receive Port. An XML document will be picked up by this port.

- Create a new Receive Port and Receive Location combination, both named Company.BizTalk.Receive.Enrollment.XML.

- Set the Type to File and point it to the directory where the XML will be dropped.

- Set the Receive Pipeline to the default XMLReceive.

File Send Port

This port, which will be associated with a BizTalk party shortly, will subscribe to all data arriving on the receive port you just configured, and will map and deliver the data. Take the following steps:

- Create one Send Port named Company.BizTalk.Send.X834.

- Set the Type to File.

- Set the Send Pipeline to EdiSend.

- On the Filters tab, set the filter to BTS.ReceivePortName == [*the name of the receive port you just configured, which is Company.BizTalk.Receive.Enrollment. XML*].

- On the Outbound Maps tab, select the map that you just deployed (Demo. BizTalk.Maps.X834).

■ **Note** You can add multiple maps to a Send Port, which will allow you to reuse it to send a variety of outbound document types. When you have multiple maps, BizTalk will iterate through each of them to see if the document that the Send Port just received matches any of the source document schemas in the maps. It will use the first map that it finds which matches this source schema.

Party Settings

You can reuse most of the party settings that you have created in previous chapters. The required components are as follows.

- Two trading partners. One representing the home organization (your company), and one for the recipient organization that the 834 EDI documents are being sent to.

- One agreements. Again, if you have configured an agreement from an earlier solution in this book, you can reuse it – just extend it to handle the 834.

- In the agreement, the key information to configure is as follows:
  - ○ The Identifiers tab must be set up on both the inbound and outbound settings.
  - ○ The Send Port tab on the outbound settings (Home Company->Trading Partner) must have a reference to the send port configured earlier in this chapter.
  - ○ The Envelope tab must have the information for the 834 transaction type configured.

    - Transaction Type should be 834-Benefit Enrollment and Maintenance.
    - Version is set to 00401 or 00501 (match your correct version).
    - Target namespace should be `http://schemas.microsoft.com/BizTalk/EDI/X12/2006`
    - GS1 should be BE-Benefit Enrollment and Maintenance (834)
    - GS2 through GS7 should be set based on what your trading partner requires (see the trading partner implementation guide or a sample 834 instance from them)
    - GS8 should be 004010 (or 005010 for 5010, you will need to match the right version).

Enabling and Running the Solution

In order for this solution to work, the Receive Location and the Send Port must be enabled. You will want to restart the BizTalk Host Instance to ensure that all of the most recent configurations and components are loaded into memory.

Conclusion

You have just configured and deployed the simplest of outbound EDI solutions. It is important to understand the core components required in an implementation. When building a solution, always think of the simplest process, and then build in the additional architectural components required by your specific implementation. You have now looked at a variety of complex (requiring multiple BizTalk components) and simple solutions. You should now have the tools and skills to develop any kind of health care EDI based solution that you may come across.

Index

Get the eBook for only $10!

Now you can take the weightless companion with you anywhere, anytime. Your purchase of this book entitles you to 3 electronic versions for only $10.

This Apress title will prove so indispensible that you'll want to carry it with you everywhere, which is why we are offering the eBook in 3 formats for only $10 if you have already purchased the print book.

Convenient and fully searchable, the PDF version enables you to easily find and copy code—or perform examples by quickly toggling between instructions and   applications. The MOBI format is ideal for your Kindle, while the ePUB can be utilized on a variety of mobile devices.

Go to www.apress.com/promo/tendollars to purchase your companion eBook.